100 YEARS
MENSWEAR

LAURENCE KING

First published in 2009
This edition published in 2012
by Laurence King Publishing Ltd
361–373 City Road
London EC1V 1LR
Tel: +44 20 7841 6900
Fax: +44 20 7841 6910
Email: enquiries@laurenceking.com
www.laurenceking.com

A catalogue record for this book is available from the British Library.

ISBN-13: 978 1 78067 021 8

Designed by Studio8 Design
Mini edition cover design by Jason Ribeiro

Printed in China

Front cover: Steve McQueen
(Globe Photos/Rex Features)

100 YEARS OF MENSWEAR

CALLY BLACKMAN

This book is a celebration of men's fashion and style – until recently, often considered secondary to women's. To a large extent, menswear of the twentieth century has been written out of the history of dress, regarded as essentially dull in comparison to the more obvious glamour of women's fashion. This perception came about partly because of the general acceptance of psychoanalyst J.C. Flügel's theory of 'the great masculine renunciation' of fashion, published in *The Psychology of Clothes* in 1930. James Laver, a respected dress historian, backed this theory in his 1937 *Taste & Fashion*, in which he claimed men were unable to compete with women in the arena of fashion from the late eighteenth century until the so-called 'peacock revolution' of the 1960s. However, long before the 1960s, men were expressing sartorial style, not only by wearing a beautifully cut suit, but also by dressing in ways that were avant-garde, daring, innovative, even subversive, and they were doing this to a much greater extent than women.

It is a fact that menswear has had a far greater influence on women's fashion over the last century than the other way round. Women have universally adopted male garments, such as suits, trousers, shirts and jeans, whereas men rarely wear dresses or skirts: sartorial boundaries predicated on gender have disappeared in favour of a wardrobe that is almost entirely based on a male model. Two of the most important components of this male-oriented wardrobe are sportswear and workwear. Both initially regarded as non-fashion, these types of clothing now dominate the wardrobes of both sexes – it is difficult to imagine a world without jeans, tracksuit bottoms or trainers, all garments that were originally worn exclusively by men.

Men are also largely responsible for introducing subcultural modes of dress, that is clothes worn by a minority to oppose or to reject the societal and sartorial norms of a dominant culture. From the 1920s undergraduate wearing his Oxford bags to the New Romantic of the 1980s, via gangsters, zoot suiters, Zazous, Teddy boys, hippies, mods and punks, male subcultural styles have had an all-pervading effect on fashion. In our now-fragmented society and kaleidoscopic culture of contemporary fashion, where anything goes, subversion or resistance through dress is no longer necessary or meaningful; the potency of this strategy has been dissipated. However, designers continue to reference historical subcultural styles in their search for inspiration.

The enduring success of the suit must also be acknowledged. Originally an exclusively male garment, the three-piece suit, introduced and formalized in the late seventeenth century, has prospered for nearly 350 years because of its unique capacity for nuance and variation. To adapt a phrase from Le Corbusier, the suit is a machine for living in, close-fitting but comfortable armour, constantly revised and reinvented to be, literally, well suited for modern daily life. It is still a key item in every fashionable man's wardrobe (and the female version in every woman's) and has recently enjoyed a dramatic renaissance, thus continuing to keep alive the ancient art of tailoring, the equivalent of haute couture for men, an art that dates back to the fourteenth century.

The suit may be the most successful and enduring fashion garment ever devised, but the beauty and attraction of its inherent subtlety has been overshadowed by the more conspicuous and attention-grabbing qualities of women's fashion (ironically, throughout history usually designed by men, another example of their influence). True, suits are about detail – the number of buttons on a jacket, the roll of a collar or the depth of a trouser turn-up – not visual stimulation, perhaps a further reason why men's fashion has been overlooked. Yet it is precisely the suit's perennial adaptability that makes it such a dynamic garment.

Men are now as vital to the fashion industry as women: the increasing proliferation of designer clothes, fragrances, cosmetics, magazines and media coverage aimed at them provides ample evidence. This has to some extent grown out of the influence of the gay community, which has always set standards of aesthetic awareness in clothes and grooming. Since the decriminalization of homosexuality, all men have been able to take pleasure not only in the consumption of fashion, but also in its dissemination through its highly sophisticated visual representation in style magazines and advertising.

Any book on fashion is a minefield. The categorization and classification of looks and styles is notoriously difficult; they are interwoven, overlapping and slippery – anomalies, omissions and repetitions are inevitable. This book is divided into two periods with different themes in each, chosen because they were important at a particular point in history; for example, sportswear is a dedicated theme in the first time-frame, but is interwoven throughout the second because the postwar infiltration of sportswear into mainstream fashion has made them inseparable.

This book is above all about men's style. Some men possess it, some do not. But whether portraits, documentary, fashion shots, or shots of fashion, the images in this book attest to the great diversity and the inventiveness of men's dress over the last century, and they demonstrate that men inhabit the fashion arena on equal terms.

10

Suit

48

Worker & Soldier

96

Player

132

Dressing Down, Dressing Up

214

Media Star

240

Culture Clubber

64

Artist & Reformer

82

Good Guy, Bad Guy

142

Rebel

178

Peacock

274

Stylist

284

Designer

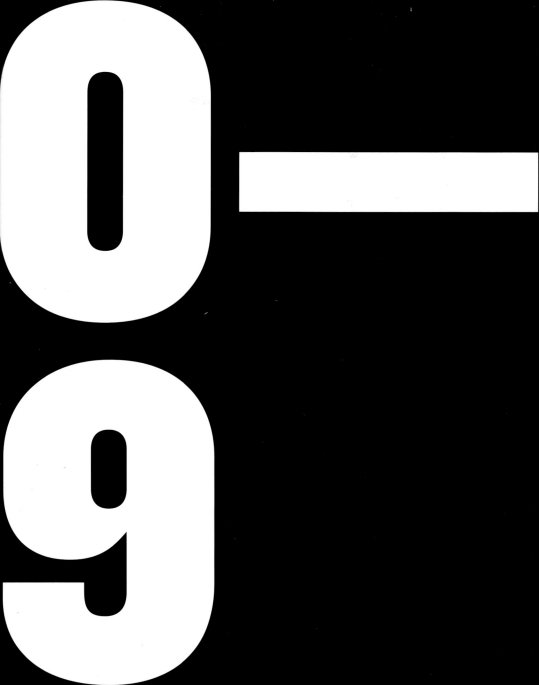

1900—1939
SUIT

Right:
Edward Prince of Wales
looking dapper in a
striped suit and socks,
with homburg, nosegay
and cane (c. 1900).

IN 1901 the Prince of Wales became Edward VII. Since his youth he had been a royal fashion icon, whose every sartorial move was closely followed by the trade and in the press, and his personal style indicated a trend towards greater informality. Rigid codes of dress were still in place, but, under Edward's influence and even before his accession, a certain esprit became the leitmotif of the Edwardian era. His heavy but considered elegance was copied, down to the twirled moustache and pointed beard. Edward adored clothes – it was rumoured that he owned the largest wardrobe in the world – while his patronage of Henry Poole from 1866 (making it the most fashionable tailor in London) ensured that a glittering international clientele, including most of the royal, aristocratic and wealthy males of Europe, America and beyond, came to London to be dressed in Savile Row.

Savile Row, a blanket term for a small collection of streets north of London's Piccadilly, had been the epicentre of the tailoring world since the early nineteenth century. At that time, Beau Brummell, the quintessential dandy, rejected foppish and over-elaborate modes of dress in favour of superb tailoring in the finest quality fabrics, making elegant understatement the fashionable goal. Brummell's influence was lasting and coincided with a period of expansion in the consumer market and the development of shopping areas such as Regent Street and its surroundings. At the same time, the gentleman's club became the focus of social activity for the fashionable male and as a consequence also the establishments that supplied the necessary commodities, from tailors to wine sellers, furnishers (suppliers of shirts and ties), hatters, bootmakers, hosiers, barbers, tobacconists, Turkish baths and tattoo parlours. Savile Row and the surrounding area had the atmosphere of a club where a man could happily pass the day, as well as earn a somewhat raffish reputation – Regent Street, Piccadilly Circus and Burlington Arcade were renowned for being the haunts of prostitutes. This was a world dominated by men for men, into which respectable women only occasionally ventured.

Poole's was one among many firms that made 'bespoke' – the tailoring of an individual by an individual – the speciality of the Row. Of course, only a few could afford their prices; most men would have patronized less expensive, local tailors and the advent of the department store from the middle of the nineteenth century increased the availability of ready-to-wear clothing. While standards of tailoring varied, the choice of garments remained the same for the upper and middle classes until after World War I: a frock coat or a morning coat for formal, semi-formal or business wear and a three-piece sack suit for informal wear and when in the country. The sack or lounge suit, as it became known, had a hip-length jacket, could be single- or double-breasted with matching waistcoat and trousers and was

rip off my tie, loosen my collar and roll up my sleeves'. Charming, handsome, easy-going and obsessed with clothes, he was immensely popular with the public, who, as with his grandfather before him, followed his every move in the world press. The Prince patronized Scholte in Savile Row, who acted as his tailor for 40 years. Scholte developed the 'London cut', a high-waisted, close-fitting suit with broad shoulders. Yet the Prince later became so enamoured with the looser American cut of trousers that he had them made in New York – 'pants across the sea' as the Duchess of Windsor called them. Described as the best-dressed man in the world, the Prince was closely scrutinized whenever he went on tours, particularly in America, where every detail of the cut of his suits, the way he tied his neckwear and the shoes he wore was reported on. This did much to bolster the reputation of London tailoring, constantly invoked in magazine editorials and advertising by the use of 'Mayfair', 'Piccadilly' and 'West End' as brand names, garment names or as fashionable background locations.

Increasingly, however, American garment manufacturers challenged London's position, helped by the country's burgeoning culture of consumption. By the 1930s, America had become the frontrunner in ready-to-wear, holiday and leisure clothing, which had grown in importance in the interwar years, despite the Wall Street Crash of 1929 and ensuing depression. Lightweight suits in cotton fabrics, such as seersucker, and belted casual jackets in linen were agreeable in the climate; trousers came in rainbow colours, short-sleeved shirts worn outside the trousers could be spotted on city streets. Even the Prince of Wales, with his love for all things American, considered Americans to be too flashily dressed at times, although he appreciated their élan. However, in terms of relaxed tailoring and ready-to-wear, America continued to gain dominance.

made in a variety of fabrics, including tweed. By the end of World War I, the frock and morning coat had become anachronisms. The lounge suit, by now more commonly called the business suit, was universally adopted for all but the most formal occasions, its loose pre-war silhouette replaced by a more streamlined version.

Whatever the style of suit, a hat was essential and was always worn until well into the second half of the twentieth century, from the formal silk top hat to the working man's cloth cap. The bowler hat, or 'coke', was usually worn with the lounge suit and became the symbol of the businessman, even into the 1960s.

The trend towards informality reflected the modern age; the zeitgeist of the 1920s called for a fresh approach to dressing, which was epitomized by the new royal fashion icon – the Prince of Wales, the future Edward VIII. Bored with tradition and with the sartorial expectations of his background, he preferred whenever alone to 'remove my coat,

Copyright 1910 by
B. Kuppenheimer & Co.

Unfailingly Correct—Unusual in Quality.

There is no satisfaction in looking less than altogether right at any time—whether it be on the promenade or in the office.

For the particular man—for the man who lays stress on the little perfections in clothes—our new models have a special attraction.

There is real distinction in the designs and patterns—artistic modeling that marks the garment of the higher order.

They offer a wide selection of the newest and best—clothes in which you can take proper pride—whether it be Easter Sunday or the days that follow.

Make sure of seeing what is correct and authoritative for spring and summer, by asking for Kuppenheimer Clothes—at the better clothiers. Send for our book, Styles for Men.

The House of Kuppenheimer
Chicago   New York   Boston

Below:
Equally suitable
for formal occasions,
though thought to
be less dressy than
the frock coat, was
the single-breasted
morning coat, with
fronts curving round
to the back, outlined
here with contrasting
binding, as is the
matching waistcoat.
Striped trousers, a
stiff collar and cuffs,
a loosely knotted tie,
pearl pin and shoes
tied with ribbon laces
lighten the effect
(c. 1900).

Right:
Lord Chesterfield
and companions at
the Epsom Derby wear
semi-formal morning
suits, overcoats,
white slips under their
waistcoats and silk
hats (1910).

Suit

Below:
Advertisement for
The Century Clothing
Company. Two 'Prince
Albert' frock coats (88,
92) attest to the lasting
fashion influence of
Edward VII. American
terminology applies: the
morning coat is called a
'cutaway frock' (90)and
the 'one-button frock' is
a morning-coat suit (94).
Older men continued to
wear these styles into
the 1920s (1916–17).

Opposite:
Pencil drawing by
Tom Purvis for Austin
Reed. A semi-formal
morning suit with
informal shirt and
tie, silk hat and gloves.
Canes had by now been
replaced by the more
useful tightly rolled
umbrella (mid 1920s).

Previous spread:
A glass lantern slide
depicting a group of
worried businessmen,
all wearing tuxedos,
so-called because they
were first worn at the
Tuxedo Park Club near
New York in the 1880s.
Having been a guest
at Sandringham where
he observed the Prince
of Wales in a short
dinner jacket, one of
the members introduced
it to the club (1906).

Right:
An illustration from
the magazine *Tailor &
Cutter* portrays formal
full evening dress: tails,
wing collar, white tie,
starched shirt front,
white piqué waistcoat,
silk stockings and
patent pumps with
bows (1902).

Left:
Vanity Fair's 'Men of the Day'. Composer Isidore de Lara in a blue velvet frogged smoking jacket – the possible inspiration for the dinner jacket or tuxedo (1908).

24

1900–1939

Suit

Right:
An advertisement for
Fashion Park, New
York, in *The Saturday
Evening Post*. The
tuxedo allowed for
greater informality:
while full evening
dress was always
worn with white
accoutrements, the
tuxedo could be worn
with black tie and
waistcoat (1921).

Below left:
An advertisement in
Country Life in America
for Cluett dress shirts.
The shirts were heavily
starched, as were the
everyday collars and
cuffs, which attached
with studs and were
easily removed for
laundering (1908).

Opposite:
Supremely elegant
full evening dress and
a dinner jacket by
Hermann Hoffmann
are shown in this plate
from the luxury German
fashion magazine *Styl*
(1922).

Below right:
Pencil drawing by Tom
Purvis for Austin Reed.
In the 1920s, the male
silhouette was more
curvaceous than the
female. Softly rounded
shoulders, a nipped-
in waist and trousers
cut full over the hips
accentuated the figure
far more than in the
early part of the century
(mid 1920s).

TAILORED AT FASHION PARK

TUX-KAY

TUX-KAY

THE FASHION PARK TUX-KAY IS AN
ENTIRELY COMFORTABLE TUXEDO, AL-
THOUGH IT HAS THE ELEGANCE RE-
QUIRED FOR SEMI-FORMAL USAGE.

ILLUSTRATED NOTES, OUTLINING THE
OCCASIONS AND ACCESSORIES WHICH
PERTAIN TO THE TUX-KAY AND ITS
USAGE, ARE AVAILABLE ON REQUEST.

CUSTOM SERVICE WITHOUT
THE ANNOYANCE OF A TRY-ON
READY-TO-PUT-ON

FASHION PARK

Rochester, New York

The smarter the function, the more promi-
nent the shirt bosom. That is but one of the
reasons why you should always select a

Cluett

DRESS SHIRT

$1.50 and more

I M C L U B
MODELLE VON HERMANN HOFFMANN
ZEICHNUNG VON KREUSCHER

Below left:
The tyranny of starch:
Charles Spencer,
6th Earl Spencer and
Liberal politician, in a
formal high round collar
and white silk cravat,
sporting a fashionable
moustache (October
1903).

Below right:
Signor Bazzini wears a
lounge suit with sloping
shoulders and a stiff,
double, turned-down
collar with loosely
knotted patterned tie.
Facial hair was going
out of fashion for the
younger, more up-to-
date man, a trend aided
by the improved safety
razor (c. 1905).

Opposite above:
An advertisement for
Arrow collars and
shirts. The Arrow Collar
Man, drawn by J.C.
Leyendecker, became
one of the world's
most successful brand
images in the early
twentieth century. The
tennis player is wearing
a buttoned-down semi-
soft collar (1912).

Opposite below:
T.M. Lewin catalogue.
Gentlemen's shirtmaker
in Jermyn Street since
1898, T.M. Lewin sold a
range of detachable stiff
collars in a variety of
styles and fabrics, some
even coloured for leisure
pursuits (1904).

T·M·Lewin

COLLARS

SPECIALITY

"QUARTER" INCH.

Sizes in Stock from

14½, 14¾, 15, 15½ up to 17

Extra Quality.

Fourfold

and Hand-made Holes.

All best and latest shapes.

FROM STOCK

10d. each, or 9/6 per doz.

TO SPECIAL ORDER

1/- each, or 11/6 per doz.

No. 300 A.X.
2½, 2¾, 2⅜

No. 301 B.
2, 2¼, 2½, 2¾

No. 302 C.
2¼, 2½, 2¾

No. 303 DX·RD. D.R
2¼, 2½

T·M·Lewin

COLLARS

Coloured "Double" Collars to order, for Motoring, Shooting, Golfing, etc.

No.		
308 Oxford	-	1/6
309 Zephyr	-	1/6
(Soft or Starched)		
310 Premier Flannel	-	1/6
311 Union	-	1/6
312 Ceylon	-	1/6
313 Indian Kashmir	-	2/
314 Silk and Kashmir		2/
315 Silk	-	2/6

The Soft Collars are made with a pocket for Stiffener

No.		
316 Stiffener	-	3d.
317 Cuffs, 1/6 per pair		
or 17/6 per dozen		

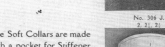

No. 304 G.
1½

No. 305 H.
2, 2¼, 2½

No. 306 J.
2, 2¼, 2½

No. 307 K.
TO ORDER ONLY.

Below:
An advertisement for
B. Stern & Son, New
York, showing a vast
array of styles. The
lounge suit and bowler
hat were increasingly
preferred to the more
formal styles seen
on either side (1906).

Opposite:
The Prince of Wales,
future George V, a
conventional dresser,
offsets the informality
of his checked lounge
suit with a formal wing
collar. He continued to
wear a frock coat well
into the 1920s, long
after it had gone out
of fashion (1901–05).

Opposite:
Mark Twain in signature
white serge 'don't give
a damn' lounge suit.
He had 14 made so that
he could wear a fresh
one each day. Possibly
referencing his southern
heritage, possibly
a political statement,
whatever his intentions
Twain cuts a dandyish
figure with a white
Ascot tie and pearl
pin (1900).

Left:
A postcard by
Alexander Bassano
shows actor Farren
Soutar in a three-piece
white lounge suit,
straw boater and white
summer shoes. A white
'duck' suit in flannel
or linen was suitable
for summer wear
and seaside holidays
(c. 1905).

1900–1939
Suit

Right:
Office clerks strolling
through Hyde Park,
London, in a heatwave.
High-cut trousers were
teamed with braces, the
usual means of support
until the late 1920s
when belts were adopted
and waistcoats began
to be abandoned.
There was a widening
distinction between
formal and informal
shirts – soft shirts with
attached collars and
cuffs were increasingly
worn, sometimes even
without a tie. The man
on the right wears a
cummerbund (May 1914).

Below:
'Gentleman' Jim Corbett,
USA heavyweight
boxing champion
renowned for his style,
accessorizes his rather
shapeless lounge suit
with a jaunty straw
boater and cane (1909).

FRÜHJAHR
ANZÜGE VON HERRMANN HOFFMANN
ZEICHNUNG VON STEPHAN KROTOWSKI

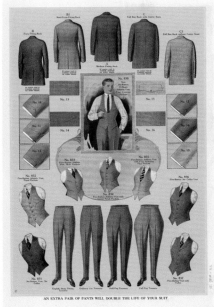

Opposite:
Plate from *Styl* magazine.
A mustard-yellow suit
with fitted waist, a
matching overcoat and
vertically striped socks
demonstrate liberation
from the monochrome
in Germany (1922).

Far left:
Advertisement for
Exclusive Fancy
Styles. Variations on
the lounge suit (still
sometimes called the
sack) continued to
be explored: fancy
styles in fancy fabrics
characterize the
American approach
to tailoring (1918–22).

Left above:
As the caption below
this advertisement
states, the life of a
suit could be greatly
extended by buying two
pairs of trousers, which
were short and tapered,
with or without turn-ups
(1918–22).

Left below:
Cover of *Monsieur*
by Maurice Taquoy.
Publishers in the 1920s
were fast becoming
aware of the increasing
demand by men for
information on fashion
and advice on how
to dress. During this
period France was in
the vanguard of luxury
fashion-magazine
publishing: *Monsieur*
ran from 1920 to 1925
and was the male
counterpart of Lucien
Vogel's seminal *La
Gazette du Bon Ton*
(1920).

36

1900–1939

Suit

Right:
Oxford bags were a
flamboyant departure
from convention and
became, in moderated
form, a widespread
fashion. They derived
their name from the
group of undergraduates
at Oxford who were
thought to have
introduced the style
(1925).

Left:
White plus fours are worn with a jacket, matching waistcoat, regimental tie and correspondent shoes (1927).

Below:
Cambridge undergraduates in plus fours. Previously only worn for country pursuits, plus fours hung over the knee with a four-inch overlap, but this allowance varied (1926).

Below left:
The Duke of Kent and
his older brother the
Prince of Wales (right)
on tour in Panama
wearing matching
lightweight striped suits
and boaters, the latter
more rakish in a bow
tie and correspondent
shoes (c. 1931).

Below right:
Fashion leader the
Prince of Wales in a
double-breasted chalk-
stripe suit with wide
lapels, a soft-collared
shirt tabbed under
the tie and a jaunty
handkerchief (1925).

Opposite:
A shop window display
demonstrates the
Prince of Wales's
selling power as a
fashion icon (c. 1931).

Below left:
Mayfair Fashions
advertise their
lightweight summer
suits with a feminine
silhouette for the seaside.
In the background, more
casual outfits can be
seen: blazers, flannels,
short-sleeved shirts,
boaters and berets
(1933).

Below right:
Cover of the first edition
of *Esquire* by Edward
Wilson. A runaway
success during the Great
Depression, *Esquire* was
published by the Hearst
Corporation. It contained
a muscular mix of racy
articles by writers such
as Ernest Hemingway,
Dashiell Hammett
and Ring Lardner, and
sophisticated illustrations
that depicted the latest
trends in fashionable
locations accompanied
by authoritative text
(1933).

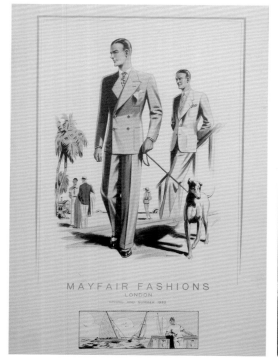

GRAY SHARKSKIN

BLUE BROADCLOTH SHIRTING

BLUE SATIN FOR TIE

BROWN GUNCLUB CHECK SAXONY

IVORY COLOR SILK SHIRTING

CLUSTER STRIPE REP TIE

Left:
An *Esquire* magazine
article about two
'British blade' suits
(meaning with a plain
back) with appropriate
swatches of cloth.
Esquire recommends
in great detail what
to wear with the
two suits and how
to accessorize (1937).

GREY SHARKSKIN *(April Esquire)* The British Blade model has added comfort—a universal appeal to all men—a powerful selling point—it therefore should be purchased and featured in all types of clothing, for semi-sports wear, for sports wear, for town and formal wear. It is shown here in a double-breasted suit suitable for town wear only. The front of this double-breasted carries four buttons instead of the usual six, and the back is plain.

Appropriate accessories for wear with this suit and suggested, to form a suitable window display ensemble, are a blue broadcloth shirt worn with a white stiff semi-widespread collar, a dark blue satin tie, pearl stickpin, grey lisle hose and black calf blucher front town shoes. Since sharkskin "can take it", the window card should suggest that the suit is appropriate for travel, as well as for in-town wear.

The second suit again reflects the trend to semi-sports wear. The brown Gun club check Saxony fabric is really a country fabric cut on town lines. It is made in a single-breasted peak lapel model with the authentic British Blade back. Accessories that are geared for fashion promotion are: the ivory color lounge collar shirt, horizontal stripe lightweight wool hose, brown calf monk front shoes, and the new cluster stripe rep silk necktie that represents a new idea from London and harmonizes with the whole costume.

Right:
Advertisement for
Mayfair Gentleman
and American Sartorial
Designer. By now the
lounge suit dominated
both formal and informal
wear. Hunting dress
and full evening wear
are also featured – a
complete wardrobe for
the modern man (1935).

123

124

101

102

106

107

108

109

110

MAYFAIR GENTLEMAN

· AND ·

AMERICAN SARTORIAL DESIGNER

LONDON

SPRING AND SUMMER EDITION, 1935

DESIGNED AND PUBLISHED BY
AMERICAN SARTORIAL DESIGNER CO.
149 WEST 36TH STREET
NEW YORK

PRINTED IN U.S.A.

Below:
Anthony Eden,
a Conservative
politician in the UK,
was considered a
fashion leader during
the 1930s, known for
his debonair elegance.
His favourite style of
homburg hat became
known as an 'Anthony
Eden' (1935).

Opposite:
Entitled 'London
Manner for Springtime
in Paris', this plate
in *Esquire* magazine
reflects Eden's fame
in America, pointing
out his homburg, white
waistcoat, gloves and
rattan cane. The caption
goes on to explain how
to Americanize the look
(1936).

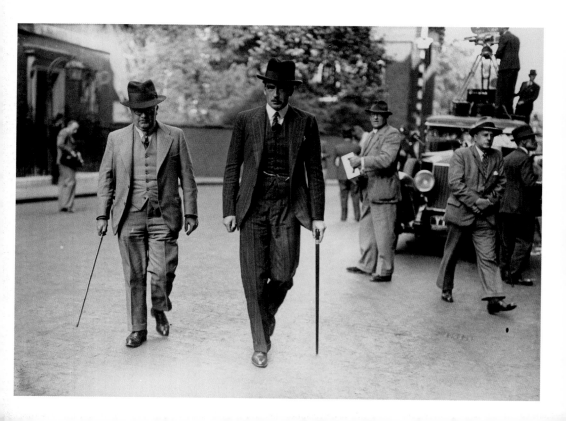

L FELLOWS

LONDON MANNER FOR SPRINGTIME IN PARIS

Anthony eden has exerted an enormous influence on continental fashions this year, as witness this turnout featuring such characteristic Eden touches as the black Homburg worn with a white linen waistcoat and white gloves. To American eyes the effect is somewhat dandified, but the Continent is always fertile ground for the dandy manner. The suit is of flannel with a faint blue overplaid. The shirt is of fine batiste with a white laundered collar, the specialty of a famous Paris shirt maker. The large knot foulard bow tie is a typical French shape which has gained London acceptance. The sack wrist gloves are lightweight white pigskin. Americanization of this outfit may involve dispensing with the white gloves and the rattan stick and substituting a soft felt or a straw hat for the Homburg. But the combination above is not too extreme for Metropolitan acceptance.

(For answers to all dress queries, send stamped self-addressed envelope to Esquire Fashion Staff, 366 Madison Ave., N. Y.)

Right:
Head cutter Mr Smith
fits a jacket at Henry
Poole in Savile Row,
which continued as
the centre of traditional
bespoke wear, but
was beginning to be
threatened by high-
street chains (1938).

Below:
Montague Burton,
'The Tailor of Taste',
became the world's
largest tailoring chain
in the 1950s. In 1939
its top-of-the-range
made-to-measure suit
cost seven guineas –
less than half the price
of one from Saville
Row (1939).

A suit of elegance and
dignity . . . a sheer
delight in wear. Carefully
cut, most skilfully
tailored in the magnificent
range of "Pinnacle"
Weaves . . . (glance at the
page opposite)

7 GUINEA VALUE
SUIT
TO MEASURE FOR 75/-

1900—1939
WORKER &
SOLDIER

50

Below:
Work clothes are often
specific to occupation.
These Calgary cowboys
wear ordinary trousers,
but the bandanas, boots,
Stetson hats, fringed
gauntlets, plaid shirt
and sheepskin chaps
leave no doubt as to
their profession (1929).

For generations, working dress simply meant the recycling of clothes until they were no longer usable. Economic necessity dictated that at the beginning of the twentieth century most working men wore an old suit, reserving their best, if they had one, for Sunday, the only day off in the week. Or they combined a jacket and waistcoat with trousers made of a tough, practical material such as corduroy. A striped collarless shirt, waistcoat, a kerchief round the neck, tough hobnail leather boots and a flat cap, or sometimes a bowler if a tie was worn, were the 'uniform' of the manual worker in Western societies.

More specific modes of dress have evolved since medieval times, when different trades and professions were marked out from each other by the clothing they wore. By the eighteenth century, the shepherd's smock frock or the lawyer's wig clearly signified the occupation of the wearer; by the late nineteenth century, not only the fisherman's occupation but also his home port could be identified by his knitted jersey. Non-military 'uniforms' can also be related to livery – the coloured clothes that marked one out as being in the service of royalty or nobility, or nowadays of a company. The dark blue of the police force, the red of the Canadian mounties or the yellow of the Automobile Association, founded in 1905, are instantly recognizable.

Workwear in our now-unstructured society is no longer as easily identified and is no longer a distinct element of the male wardrobe. Seismic changes in societal norms and dress codes since the beginning of the twentieth century have meant that office workers in open-necked shirts and shorts can be seen on the streets of Manhattan and doctors no longer wear white coats. Many items formerly associated only with workwear have entered the mainstream wardrobe, from construction workers' boots to hardy textiles such as corduroy. But one item of workwear in particular dominates clothing globally: denim jeans, which ironically now symbolize leisure rather than work. Their phenomenal success can be traced from the mid-nineteenth century, with prospectors in the Gold Rush through to construction workers building skyscrapers in New York in the 1910s and 1920s, and on to teenagers in the 1950s and ever since. Their hardwearing qualities, combined with their comfort, ensured universal popularity by the

Far left:
Irish writer James
Joyce, aged 22, wearing
the typical working-
man's outfit of ill-fitting
lounge-suit jacket,
waistcoat and contrasting
trousers, a stiff collar,
tie and flat cap (1904).

Left:
An Automobile
Association scout
displays the new
uniform of a short,
waterproof double-
breasted jacket,
jodhpurs and a smart
peaked cap. Even
an outdoor job like his
called for a high, stiffened
collar. Methods of
waterproofing fabric
steadily improved (1909).

last quarter of the twentieth century and subjected them to endless variations of styling by designers – the classic example of workwear becoming designer wear.

Today's 'sea of denim' can be compared to the 'sea of khaki' that spread from America to Australia after the outbreak of World War I in 1914. The loss of a generation of young men caused a societal shift resulting in the disruption of the rigid social hierarchy that had previously dictated sartorial codes. Fashion began to be democratized as society adjusted itself to the influence of socialist politics: better housing and working conditions, wider availability of commodities and greater choice. Postwar economic recovery was faster in America. Mass production of uniforms resulted in streamlined manufacture, standardization of sizing and the unionization of workers in the clothing trades, establishing the springboard for America's giant garment-manufacturing industry.

At the outbreak of World War II, the urbane glamour of the 1930s gave way to more sombre considerations. The output of textiles and clothing manufacture was once again channelled into kitting out the forces. Civilian clothing was stringently rationed. In Britain, the coupon system, introduced in 1941 and continued until 1949, provided men with 66 coupons in the first year (a number that subsequently decreased): with jacket, trousers and waistcoat amounting to 26 coupons, there was very little room for purchasing other than basic requirements. Details that used too much fabric, such as trouser turn-ups and pocket flaps, were banned, while designers were commissioned to come up with utility clothing that adhered to such restrictions.

Clothes rationing was also introduced in France where shortages of raw materials quickly became acute, boosting the second-hand clothing trade. During occupation, the French garment industry was commandeered to supply Germany with high-end and military clothing, despite losing much of its skilled Jewish workforce to the concentration camps. America too limited its consumption of fabrics after Pearl Harbor in 1941. With wool mainly reserved for uniforms, cotton and synthetic fabrics, such as rayon, viscose and nylon, were increasingly used for civilian wear. When peace was declared in 1945, soldiers in Britain were issued with a demob suit of civilian clothes from menswear chain Montague Burton – one of the first high-street stores to modernize their retail outlets after the war and to introduce improved standards of tailoring for the mass market.

Many items of uniform have travelled into the fashionable mainstream (in the late 1940s and early 1950s, much of it via the black market). Airforce bomber jackets, Navy duffel coats and heavy-knit sailors' sweaters were taken up by youths who weere lucky enough not to have had to wear them, some making them into symbols of resistance against conventional society along the way – and they remain fashion classics today. A more recent example of the appropriation of uniform by fashion is the use of camouflage, now visible not only on the battlefield, but on the high street, from trousers to underwear to forage caps (yet another item of military uniform).

Blue Buckle OverAlls
Union Made

"Strong-for-Work!"

Greater wear value and comfort couldn't be put into a work garment than you buy in every pair of Blue Buckles! They are built to do a great job! That's why Blue Buckles are *the quality standard overall of America!*

Every engineer, farmer, mechanic, home-gardener, garage worker, motorist—every man with a real job to do—will delight in Blue Buckles' big, generous "over-size." Roomy coats have those bully free-sway raglan sleeves!

Blue Buckles solid reinforced backband eliminates the old style, ever ripping V-shaped vent; fly is *cut into* the overall, not made separately and sewed on; big-capacity pockets, and a lot of them; solid brass fittings that defy rust —and the highest grade workmanship to assure very unusual wear service and satisfaction. Blue Buckles well repay your closest inspection—*and your confidence!*

Dealers who have not yet been able to secure Blue Buckle OverAlls should write their nearest jobber at once.

Jobbers OverAll Company, Inc., Lynchburg, Va.   *Selling Agents:* W. T. Stewart Dept., Leonard Sales Co., 64 Leonard St., New York

Opposite:
Advertisement for Blue
Buckle OverAlls. The
American blue-collar
worker had worn denim
since Levi Strauss,
whose name has
become synonymous
with jeans, started
making jeans for miners
in the California Gold
Rush of the 1850s. The
campaign hat worn on
the left is a remnant
from World War I (1919).

Left:
Matinée idol Gary
Cooper in a soft cotton
shirt with sleeves
rolled up, a style long
associated with manual
labour and a sartorial
metaphor for getting
down to work (1930).

Opposite:
New recruits to the
army wearing jodhpurs
and puttees, long
worn in the tropics for
protection and highly
practical in the muddy
trenches. The high-
quality fabrics and
comparative elegance
of the uniform must
have been a revelation
for many (1914).

Below:
Soldiers arrive home
on leave for Christmas
armed with mistletoe.
The military overcoat,
or 'British warm',
proved so popular
that it continued in use
long after World War I
(December 1915).

Opposite:
Advertisement for
Burberry's trench
coat. Adapted from
Burberry's Tielocken
worn during the
Boer War, the trench
coat was made of
waterproofed gaberdine.
Officers could have a
complete set of uniform
made within four days
(1918).

Left:
The trench coat, future
staple of the male
wardrobe, was belted
and double-breasted
with a large collar,
gun flap, epaulettes
and cuffs that could be
cinched. As the tough
guy of Hollywood,
Humphrey Bogart gave
it the seal of approval,
and as a versatile cover-
up, it became associated
with underworld
activities (1942).

Below:
Gunners in the British
navy wearing duffel
coats, a military garment
whose popularity lasted
long after the war. Its
toggle–loop fastenings
were easier to do up
when wearing gloves
on the Arctic convoys
(c. 1943).

Opposite above:
Advertisement for
Viyella. Garment
manufacturers were
obliged to supply forces
rather than civilians
during wartime, as this
advertisement makes
clear (1940s).

Opposite below:
Pilots wearing leather
bomber jackets, one
lined with sheepskin,
another item of military
wear that passed into
fashion (1944).

Following spread:
Communist leader Mao
Zedong inspects troops
during the China–Japan
War wearing the famous
suit that was advocated,
though not prescribed.
It evolved from the
design by Sun Yat-sen
in the early twentieth
century and came into
use in the West in the
1960s, worn by students
in countercultural
movements, especially
in Paris (1944).

THE NAME TO REMEMBER IN...

WAR AND PEACE

We regret that 'Viyella' is no longer available for civilians at home, as the Fighting Forces have first call on this famous cloth.

'Viyella' for Men

OVERSEAS OFFICES AND REPRESENTATIVES THROUGHOUT THE WORLD

Below:
Fidel Castro and Che
Guevara in Cuba. Che's
bearded face and beret
with the star pin have
become the symbolic
image of revolution
worldwide (1960).

Opposite above:
Two outfits that
demonstrate the impact
of the war in America.
A cosy all-in-one
checked flannel air-raid
outfit (left) with matching
bow tie and useful
pockets for essential
items echoes Winston
Churchill's famous
siren suit. A 'Life' suit
(right) modelled in the
Waldorf lobby, with
all superfluous fabric
eliminated (collar,
pocket flaps and trouser
turn-ups), strictly
adheres to rationing
regulations (1942).

Opposite below left:
A 'Superior' suit on
the left looks far more
modern than the
standard government-
issue demob suit on
the right. These were
made by high-street
firms such as Montague
Burton, giving rise
to the slang for a suit:
a monty (1945).

Opposite below right:
A GI looks at a selection
of civilian clothing;
the style of the suit is
exactly the same as
before World War II
(July 1945).

1900—1939
ARTIST &
REFORMER

Right:
Augustus John
cultivated his bohemian
image by wearing
earrings, long hair,
an unkempt beard and
unconventional clothes.
Here he stands by the
gypsy caravan in which
he and his extended
family lived and
travelled for some time,
emulating the lifestyle
of Romany Gypsies
(c. 1905).

Artists of every kind tend to be in the vanguard of fashion, or choose to dress differently – a by-product of the self-belief required to pursue their profession, of the avant-garde milieu they inhabit and its disregard for convention and of a certain indulgence, if not expectation, on the part of the public to be shocked by them. Since the early nineteenth century, the cult of the artist-as-genius flourished, leading to the self-conscious promotion of an 'artistic' image. Augustus John's carefully cultivated bohemian dress matched his bohemian lifestyle, while his fellow artist in Paris, Pablo Picasso, adopted the working-man's uniform of a jean or corduroy suit, no doubt through economic necessity, but also perhaps as a self-identification with the working man (ironically apposite to the idea of genius).

Politics, art and fashion are close companions, and aesthetic, artistic and rational attempts to reform dress are similarly closely linked and overlapping. Since the Pre-Raphaelites, artists have endeavoured to wear clothes that are simultaneously beautiful and not harmful: attempts to reform dress multiplied in the mid-nineteenth century as fashion dictated increasingly contorted and restricted modes (men were not averse to wearing corsets at this time). Dr Jaeger of Stuttgart founded an empire on the premise that only wool should be worn next to the skin, as it encouraged the passage of toxins through perspiration. George Bernard Shaw throughout his long life was an enthusiastic disciple of Dr Jaeger and took woollen sheets with him whenever visiting or travelling. The Men's Dress Reform Party, established in 1929, tried to make improvements, but these efforts were subsumed by World War II and never regained currency: ultimately reform became irrelevant as casual, sports and subcultural dress became the driving forces of change.

Many of the artistic movements active in the years before World War I made dress design part of their manifesto. The Vienna Secessionists and their colleagues at the Wiener Werkstätte integrated all aspects of art, architecture and design, including clothes, which they produced to coordinate with furniture and interiors. Much of this output was done by, and directed at, women. It was the Futurists in Italy (exclusively male) who designed colourful, modifiable men's suits, waistcoats and ties exploding with vortices of pattern that expressed modernity and celebrated the dynamism of urban life. Ernesto Michahelles (known as Thayaht) designed the *tuta*, practical overalls for men and women, garments for a utopian future without fashion, which the Futurists ostensibly despised, while the Russian Constructivists' political agenda required production of utilitarian clothing for the masses. In post-revolutionary Russia, art was declared 'dead', the artist's new role was now to *produce* tangible objects rather than to *create* abstract ideas. In Paris, Sonia Delaunay applied her art to clothes,

Above:
Lifelong rational
dresser and vegetarian,
playwright George
Bernard Shaw in
a stockinette suit
especially made for
him by Jaeger (1886).

stitching wearable garments for both sexes that were moving tapestries of Simultaneist art. Later the Surrealists made clothes *as* art, from Salvador Dali's 1936 dinner jacket adorned with drinking glasses containing green liquid, via Joseph Beuys's 1970 conceptual *Felt Suit* symbolizing protective armour, to Leigh Bowery's outrageous shape-shifting costumes for his performance art during the 1980s and early 1990s, and this practice continues today.

As with workwear, artistic dress as a distinct phenomenon is no longer identifiable in a culture where anything goes, but the influence of those who designed it and the brave souls who wore it in the years before World War II is significant. It heralded the now intimate relationship between fashion and the arts and bolstered the concept of fashion designer as artist, an idea that has resulted in today's regular displays of fashion designers' work in all the major museums of the world. Whether from the self-conscious desire to declare their profession (and genius) as an artist through dress, making a visible statement of political and/or artistic ideology, or using clothes to *make* art through image-making, construction, conceptual or performance, art and fashion are now inseparable.

68

Artist &
Reformer

Right above:
Pablo Picasso wears
a working-man's suit,
possibly of jean, a
hard-wearing cotton
fabric woven in Nîmes.
The origin of the word
denim comes from this:
de Nîmes (1912).

Right below:
Rupert Brooke's
coloured shirt with
soft collar, loosely
knotted 'artistic' scarf
tie and long hair project
modernity and youth.
They also suggest
socialist leanings,
as coloured shirts were
only worn by working-
class men before World
War I (1913).

Opposite:
Italian-born artist
Amedeo Modigliani
presents an
astonishingly modern
image in an open-neck
shirt and velour
collared sweater (1909).

Artist &
Reformer

Below and right:
One of the founder
members of the Vienna
Succession, Gustav
Klimt was closely
connected with the
Wiener Werkstätte,
a cooperative of artist-
craftsmen that aimed
to integrate the fine
and decorative arts,
including fashion. It
is not known whether
Klimt designed clothes;
he was certainly
closely involved in the
promotion and branding
of his partner Emilie
Flöge's fashion house.
His depictions of clothes
and fabrics, many
designed by the Wiener
Werkstätte, show great
sensitivity towards
dress. Nicknamed 'the
athlete' by his friends,
he preferred, when
working, among friends
or on summer holidays
at the lakes, to wear a
full-length indigo-dyed
smock, embroidered
with white linen motifs
(below), with nothing
underneath. For him,
it symbolized freedom
and a return to the
simple life (c. 1910).

IL VESTITO ANTINEUTRALE

Manifesto futurista

**Glorifichiamo la guerra,
sola igiene del mondo.**
MARINETTI.
(1° Manifesto del Futurismo - 20 Febbraio 1909)

Viva Asinari di Bernezzo!
MARINETTI.
(1ª Serata futurista - Teatro Lirico, Milano, Febbraio 1910)

L'umanità si vestì sempre di **quiete**, di **paura**, di **cautela** o d'**indecisione**, portò sempre il lutto, o il piviale, o il mantello. Il corpo dell'uomo fu sempre diminuito da sfumature e da tinte **neutre**, avvilito dal nero, soffocato da cinture, imprigionato da panneggiamenti.

Fino ad oggi gli uomini usarono abiti di colori e forme statiche, cioè drappeggiati, solenni, gravi, incomodi e sacerdotali. Erano espressioni di timidezza, di malinconia e di **schiavitù**, negazione della vita muscolare, che soffocava in un passatismo anti-igienico di stoffe troppo pesanti e di mezze tinte tediose, effeminate o decadenti. Tonalità e ritmi di **pace desolante,** funeraria e deprimente.

OGGI vogliamo abolire:

1. — Tutte le tinte **neutre**, « carine », sbiadite, *fantasia*, semioscure e umilianti.

2. — Tutte le tinte e le foggie pedanti, professorali e teutoniche. I disegni a righe, a quadretti, a **puntini diplomatici.**

3. — I vestiti da lutto, nemmeno adatti per i becchini. Le morti eroiche non devono essere compiante, ma ricordate con vestiti rossi.

4. — L'equilibrio **mediocrista**, il cosidetto buon gusto e la cosidetta armonia di tinte e di forme, che frenano gli entusiasmi e rallentano il passo.

5. — La simmetria nel taglio, le linee **statiche,** che stancano, deprimono, contristano, legano i muscoli; l'uniformità di goffi risvolti e tutte le cincischiature. I bottoni inutili. I colletti e i polsini inamidati.

Noi futuristi vogliamo liberare la nostra razza da ogni **neutralità**, dall'indecisione paurosa e quietista, dal pessimismo negatore e dall'inerzia

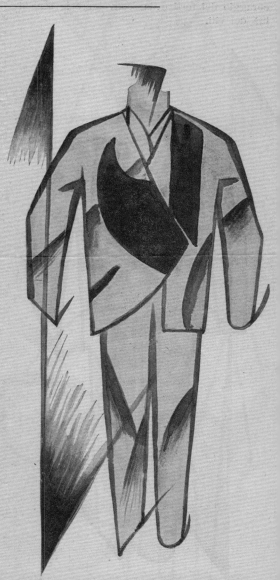

**Vestito bianco - rosso - verde
del parolibero futurista Marinetti.** *(Mattino)*

Opposite:
On 20 May 1914, Giacomo Balla published 'The Futurist Manifesto of Men's Clothing'. Neutral and pedantic colours, mourning, striped, checked or spotted fabrics, mediocrity, so-called harmony, symmetry and uniformity were abolished. In their place clothes should be aggressive, nimble, dynamic, simple, comfortable, hygienic and variable (1914).

Left:
Three projects for Futurist suits by Balla, whose aim was to make clothes variable by incorporating 'modifiers'. These appliquéd pieces of cloth of differing size, thickness or colour could be attached by 'pneumatic' buttons to transform the suit, and could also be perfumed (1914).

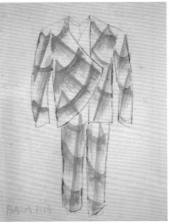

Below:
Ernesto Michahelles
(known as Thayaht)
designed, and is seen
here wearing, the *tuta*,
so-called because its
silhouette resembles a
T, from *tutta*, the Italian
for 'all'. It was simple to
make, with no decorative
details or curved
edges, only requiring
4.5 metres (15 feet) of
inexpensive cotton or
hemp fabric and seven
buttons (c. 1920).

Opposite:
The *tuta* was the ultimate
exercise in hygiene,
economy, practicality
and universality,
but it was not unisex.
Thayaht also designed
a female version, with a
skirt instead of trousers,
in the hope of reforming
the untidiness of women's
clothes. Thayaht went on
to design and illustrate
clothes for the Paris
couturière Madeleine
Vionnet (1919).

FOT. P. SALVI
FIRENZE

MODELLO DI TUTA

"VESTITO UNIVERSALE" TUTTO DI UN PEZZO

.THAYAHT.

Artist &
Reformer

Below:
Waistcoat designed by
Fortunato Depero, who
in the late 1920s went
to New York where he
designed household
furnishings and worked
as a fashion illustrator,
notably for American
Vogue (1924).

Opposite:
The Futurists published
several manifestos
on dress during their
mission to abolish
fashion, which they
regarded as evil, and
replace it with wearable
works of art capable
of constant renewal.
Filippo Marinetti and
others published 'The
Futurist Manifesto of
the Italian Hat' in 1933
in which they listed
20 different styles
of hats for various
occasions, including
a 'poetic', a 'publicity',
a 'therapeutic' (infused
with camphor and
menthol) and a 'light-
signalling' design.
Here Marinetti (right)
and Depero wear
waistcoats designed
by the latter (1924).

Page 78:
Leading Constructivist
Aleksandr Rodchenko
designed himself a work
suit, made by his wife
Varvara Stepanova in
wool and leather on her
Singer sewing machine.
With plenty of useful
pockets to hold pencils
and other tools, it
fulfilled the criteria for
a 'production dress', or
prozodezhda, a garment
perfectly adapted to the
needs of the wearer's
profession (1922).

НОВЫЙ БЫТ

Отдел материальной культуры при музее Художественной культуры Ленинграда, ведя исследовательскую работу в области изыскания новых форм, одной из основных своих вех постоянных опытов не результативной быта.

В основе этой работы—максимум жизненности и простейших, окружающих нас вещей. Художники должны организовать участвовать, в создании новой вещи, а не только пользоваться ставшими вещами. В самом в этом Отдел вырабатка задачи и уже указал, даже выставить образцы одежды, мебель, осветительных приборов, мебель и т.п. На характерные этих образцов мы остановимся.

Характерных черт в данного направление указать следующих несколько расширения в плечах и торсе (корытце) и сужения книзу форма создает следующих качества: тело выделяется силу, материал не обжимает тела и оставляет вокруг нужно прослойку,—с одной стороны, удерживая живая этим лучшие тепло принцип двойной так, с другой создает более свободное тело.

Покрой сделан с таким расчет, чтобы движение человека в нем не стеснены и даже возможность...

[текст частично неразборчив]

[рукописные примечания:]

Эта одежда отвечает техническим не механическим и носят её поэтому что называется—красивой.

О.М.К. ДЕЛАЕТ ИЗЫСКАНИЯ
НОВОЙ ФОРМЫ ПОВСЕДНЕВНОЙ
НОРМАЛЬ-ОДЕЖДЫ

Artist &
Reformer

Page 79:
Krasnaia Panorama, an illustrated journal on art and literature. The creative role of the artist in post-revolutionary Russia was abolished in favour of the production of objects: fashion was seen to be a signifier of class, and therefore anti-Communist. Vladimir Tatlin, the founder of Constructivism, designed a modular overcoat made of waterproof cloth with removable linings, one of flannel and one of fur for the winter. Under the banner 'Normal Dress', the photomontage depicts Tatlin in his overcoat and, below, in a suit that literally and metaphorically tramples over two bourgeois examples (1924).

Below left:
Tsuguharu Foujita, a Japanese artist living in Paris, creates a startling image by combining a collarless peasant print shirt with a jacquard-knit cardigan jacket (c. 1924).

Below right:
The Men's Dress Reform Party was founded in 1929 by a group of British clerics, doctors, artists and scholars and soon had branches worldwide. Members objected to collars and ties, trousers, hats and shoes, preferring sandals. It had some considerable success, including influencing the outfits worn by the BBC Promenade Orchestra in 1931: 'soft shirts and black Palm Beach jackets'. Publicity included a short film televised by the BBC in 1937, the year that the group disbanded. Dr Jordan, the Hon. Secretary of the MDRP, designed these uniforms for telegraph boys for a competition held in the same year (July 1937).

Opposite:
Tristan Tzara, painted by Robert Delaunay. Delaunay and his Russian wife, Sonia, explored kinetics and dynamic effects through the use of colour and shape. Here Tzara, one of the founders of the Dada movement, wears a 'simultaneous' scarf designed by Sonia (1923).

1900—1939
GOOD GUY, BAD GUY

Below left:
Gary Cooper in a white
summer suit and scarf,
probably not made by
Lesley & Taylor, his
London tailor (1932).

Below right:
Oscar-winning costume
designer Edith Head
called Cary Grant 'the
most elegant man I have
ever met'. Here in casual
sweater and slacks,
Grant had a passion for
clothes and later in his
career tried his hand
at running a menswear
boutique (1930s).

Opposite:
Rudolph Valentino,
leading screen sex
symbol of the 1920s,
relaxes in a tweed
three-piece smoking
suit with black cuffs and
shawl collar. Striped
socks and shiny black
Oxfords complete the
matinée idol's ensemble
(1925).

Since the mid-nineteenth century, women's fashion had been dictated by Parisian couture and men's by London tailors. However, the hegemony of European codes of dress was to be increasingly challenged by the American apparel manufacturers, one of whose greatest assets was the Hollywood movie industry. During the interwar period, cinema-going was one of the most popular forms of entertainment, creating celebrities whose images and clothes were avidly followed on- and off-screen in magazines across the world. Women swooned at the exotic looks of Rudolph Valentino, particularly when he played costume roles such as *The Sheik* in 1921, and mass hysteria broke out at his funeral five years later. The 'Latin Lover's' perfect profile, accentuated by his slicked-back hair, resulted in any imitator being called a 'Vaselino'. However, his sexuality was questioned in the press, where he was also accused of being responsible for the 'feminization' of the American male. No such accusation could be levelled at Errol Flynn, who despite acting out most of his roles in dubious costumes, maintained an impressive reputation as a ladies' man; or Gary Cooper, the archetypal blue-collar, blue-eyed hero whose reserved persona as sheriff, cowboy or soldier was again diametrically opposite to that of Flynn.

One of the most stylish stars was Cary Grant who, though born in England, achieved fame in Hollywood. On- or off-screen, his casual elegance was apparent, whether dressed in an immaculate suit by his Savile Row tailor Kilgour, French & Stanbury, or in sweater and slacks. At this time,

leading men supplied their own wardrobes, many, like Grant, heading to Savile Row for bespoke suits.

Fred Astaire, appearing on stage in London for the first time in 1923, was paid a visit in his dressing room by the Prince of Wales, whose white evening waistcoat made an indelible impression on the dancer, so much so that he had a copy made in Jermyn Street. But it is difficult to believe that anyone could look more elegant than Astaire in top hat and tails as he glided across the screen.

The movie stars who bought their suits in Savile Row gave British tailoring a boost, but others remained loyal to their own country's aesthetic. Clark Gable favoured American tailoring, less understated than British and with a looser cut: a boxy jacket with broad shoulders, wide lapels and roomy trousers. Coloured shirts, spectator shoes, a wide patterned tie and a snapped-brim hat, preferably a Borsalino, became an iconic Hollywood look associated with the dandy gangster, stemming from racketeers and Chicago Mafiosi, whose swagger in the public imagination and, to an extent, in reality, had a certain appealing cachet. George Raft and James Cagney made pinstripes look menacing, while Humphrey Bogart immortalized the trench coat. In Britain, the gangster style was taken up by the spiv, easily identified by his flashy suit, his too-wide picture tie and his too-thin pencil moustache. In France, 'swells', pimps and underworld hoodlums, otherwise known as 'les durs' (the tough guys), typically from Corsica by way of Marseilles, favoured silk shirts, quantities of gold jewelry, coloured hats that matched the loud check of their suit and pointed shoes a size too small.

Below:
Clark Gable and Jack
Benny on the set of
China Seas. Gable's
wide-shouldered, half-
belted jacket with patch
pockets, his patterned
tie and white bucks
are all unmistakably
American (1935).

Opposite:
A shop window in
Montevideo displays a
Clark Gable cardboard
cut-out modelling a
casual blouson jacket
(1941).

No. 409X   No. 441   No. 176   No. 340   No. 411
The DRAKE   *The* AVENUE   *The* SAVOY   *The* WINDSOR   *The* DRAKE

"None but Nunn-Bush for me!"

Ankle-fashioning DOES FOR SHOES WHAT HAND-TAILORING DOES FOR CLOTHES!

Most people agree that hand-tailoring makes clothes keep their shape longer, and look good for extra months of wear. Nunn-Bush shoes are ANKLE-FASHIONED to achieve the same results. This Nunn-Bush feature retards gaping and bulging at the ankle. Style lasts *longer.* Fit and comfort *endure.* You'll like the difference Ankle-fashioning makes . . . . See your Nunn-Bush dealer. MOST STYLES $8.50 *to* $11.50 *A FEW HIGHER*

Nunn-Bush
Ankle fashioned Oxfords

NUNN-BUSH SHOE CO., Milwaukee, New York, San Francisco.

No. 118   No. 499   No. 110   No. 461   No. 406
The SAVOY   *The* DRAKE   *The* SHELTON   *The* SHELTON   *The* STANFORD

Below left:
Whatever he wore, singer and dancer Fred Astaire was the epitome of debonair elegance on- and off-screen. When in casual mode, as here in rehearsal, he looks stylish in slacks, an open-necked shirt and a tie instead of a belt. Though shown wearing white canvas bucks, he popularized correspondent shoes (1936).

Below right:
Cover of the men's magazine *Adam* by Ernst Dryden. A casual short-sleeved shirt, cravat and trousers with tie belt suggest Fred Astaire style. Published in France and Britain by Condé Nast, *Adam* ran from the early 1930s until the late 1980s under various titles (1932).

Opposite:
As he is best remembered in immaculate top hat and tails, Fred Astaire is putting on the ritz in the movie *Blue Skies* (1946).

Good Guy,
Bad Guy

Right:
An advertisement for
Knapp felt hats in *The
Saturday Evening Post.*
A snapped-brim trilby
with a wide silk band
was an essential part
of the gangster look
(1930).

Below left:
George Raft's career
blossomed after his
convincing portrayal
in *Scarface* – he was
known to have friends
within the criminal
community. Considered
to be one of Hollywood's
most stylish dressers,
here Raft wears a wide-
shouldered, double-
breasted suit jacket
that is so tight it strains
across his chest.
A soft, pinned collar,
silk tie and pocket
handkerchief complete
the dapper dandy's
outfit (1932).

Opposite:
Presumably the pleat
in the back of the jacket
allowed extra ease
when using a machine
gun (late 1920s).

Below right:
James Cagney and
Humphrey Bogart
epitomize the gangster
look for their roles in
The Roaring Twenties,
a movie about
bootlegging during
Prohibition (1939).

The KNAPP-FELT *Ariel*
TEN DOLLARS
THE NEW C&K HAT OF THE MONTH
MADE BY THE CROFUT & KNAPP CO., FIFTH AVENUE, NEW YORK

Good Guy,
Bad Guy

Right:
An advertisement for
colourful patterned ties
(1940s).

Below:
On the set for *I Believe
in You*, set against a
backdrop of a bomb-
damaged London
still under rationing,
Laurence Harvey
(centre), Cyril Waites
and Stanley Escane
play small-time crooks
in costumes directly
inspired by gangsters
in American movies
(1952).

Opposite:
George Elms, described
as a spiv, poses in an
American-style suit
with very wide lapels
and a trilby. Fortunes
were made on the
black market during
and immediately after
the war by trading in
desirable commodities
that were rationed or
otherwise unobtainable,
such as silk stockings.
The spiv was associated
with this criminal
activity and was
identifiable by his flashy
dress (August 1947).

1900—1939
PLAYER

Sportswear has been the single most important influence on fashion during the twentieth century. From the baseball cap to the trainer, from the knitted sweater to the rugby shirt, sportswear has infiltrated nearly all areas of life. The absorption of sportswear into fashion gathered pace from the end of the previous century, when improvements in lifestyle and increasing leisure time fostered a craze for sporting activities and exercise through which an athletic physique became both morally and aesthetically desirable. The striped blazer and white flannel trousers worn by tennis and cricket players were acceptable as informal dress away from the court and the pitch by the first decade of the twentieth century. Plus fours, previously only worn for golf

and derived from the knickerbocker suits of the Victorians, became a fashionable alternative to trousers in the 1920s, even in town. In fact, the Prince of Wales (Edward VIII) often wore them on informal occasions as well as on the links, where he teamed them with a jazzy Fair Isle jumper. Sweaters, previously only worn by sportsmen and children, satisfied the knitting craze of the 1920s, generated in some measure by the impetus of knitting for the troops during World War I. Leather coats, some lined with sheepskin, were initially only worn by motorists and aviators for warmth and for protection from the elements, dust and engine oil in exposed driving seats and cockpits.

The immense popularity in North America of baseball, basketball and ice hockey resulted in garments such as sweatshirts, sweatpants, baseball jackets and boots infiltrating everyday wear. In the same way as movie stars, successful sportsmen became international celebrities, and many of them endorsed products. The world of sport became increasingly commercialized, inseparably linked with sponsorship and high finance.

Riding clothes, too, influenced fashion: the polo-neck sweater and the polo shirt are now wardrobe staples. Garments for sport are traditionally made in knitted jersey fabrics, as opposed to woven fabrics, giving them stretch and ease. When rubber elastic and then spandex yarns were added they became unbeatable as the ultimate in comfort for leisurewear, and now constitute a high percentage of the fabric of our wardrobes.

Left:
Garments originally
worn only for sports
or leisure activities
became increasingly
popular as sartorial
rules relaxed in the
interwar period. Here,
plus fours, Fair Isle
sweaters and argyle
socks are worn by
spectators at a sporting
event (1926).

America was the leader in innovative textile
technology through the development of jersey
fabrics and the introduction of Lycra, a type
of spandex yarn, patented by DuPont in 1958.
(Nylon, which strengthened men's hosiery
and, incidentally, the attraction of the GI during
World War II, had been patented by DuPont in
1935.) These new textile components improved
the stretch, fit and recovery qualities of ski- and
swimwear, for example, allowing US company
Jantzen to become the world leader in streamlined
bathing kit during the 1930s, a position since
challenged by a host of Australian manufacturers
who have cornered the market in swim, surf and
beach wear.

Dedicated sportswear continues to be refined
to enhance its wearer's performance. Techno
textiles have produced swimsuits made from
nylon/elastane fabrics, based on the properties of
shark skin, that are ultra-light, chlorine-resistant,
quick-drying and reduce drag; running gear
that is aerodynamic and wicks perspiration; and
gym vests that support or actually make muscles
work harder.

The relationship between sportswear
and fashion is now a two-way process. The
appropriation and customization of sportswear by
youth cultures have resulted in superbrands such
as Nike and Adidas employing 'coolhunters' to
track the latest trends on the street, while fashion
designers collaborate in crossover ventures such
as Yohji Yamamoto's Y-3 trainers for Adidas, and
sports megastar David Beckham's adverts for
Armani underpants.

Right above:
Tailor & Cutter. By popularizing the kilt and tweed ensemble for country pursuits, Edward VII continued the Highland cult started by his mother, Queen Victoria (1905).

Right below:
The Norfolk jacket was belted and had a box pleat at centre back and two at the front, one of which concealed a pocket. It was favoured by Edward VII as a roomier alternative to the lounge-suit jacket for shooting at Sandringham (hence the name Norfolk) (c. 1900).

Opposite:
The men at the back of this shooting party wear knickerbocker suits, while the man at the front sports a Norfolk jacket. They all wear protective gaiters and tweed caps or hats (c. 1905).

Opposite:
Col. Langford Brooke,
Master of the Hunt,
in hunting pink and
cord jodhpurs. A kind
of livery or uniform,
it has changed little
since the Colonel's
day and continues to
be purchased bespoke
from tailors (1902).

Below:
Plate from *American
Gentleman*. Servants in
livery in the background
attend to gentlemen
wearing hunting pink,
tweed knickerbocker
suits and driving coats.
After World War I,
the kind of lifestyle
represented here only
continued for a few of
the very wealthy elite
(1908).

American Gentleman

AUTUMN AND WINTER

Below left:
Advertisement by
Pierre Brissaud for
La Belle Jardinière,
a fashionable Parisian
store that specialized
in a wide variety of
ready-made clothing,
including, as shown
here, travelling,
hunting, sports and
livery pieces. Then,
as now, magazines
depended heavily
on advertising (1922).

Opposite:
Advertisement for
Hermann Scherrer
hunting clothes in
Germany (1927).

Below right:
Clark Gable had the
ideal figure for the
glamour of riding
clothes. Here he wears
a polo neck, another
garment that made the
transition from sports
to everyday wear (1932).

Below:
Leather coats were
practical for motoring
because they did not
absorb dust, while
goggles, hats and
gauntlet gloves were
essential. A balaclava
adds extra protection
from the elements
(1900).

Left:

Sir Henry Segrave 1896–1930 by A.H. Collins. As motor racing became popular, more specialist streamlined protective clothing, such as these overalls, was necessary. Worn by motor and aviation mechanics, overalls were adopted by World War I pilots as summer wear. The zip was patented in 1923 and made putting on and taking off clothes much quicker and more convenient. Hats were replaced by helmets and goggles protected the eyes (c. 1929).

Right:
Brazilian aviation
pioneer Alberto
Santos-Dumont wears
a collarless jean suit
with a stiff collared
shirt, a spotted silk
tie and the panama
hat that caused
much amusement
among Parisians who
witnessed his attempts
at flying dirigibles
and aircraft in the first
decade of the twentieth
century (1906).

Opposite:
The blouson-style
jacket, part military,
part sportswear,
became popular
after extensive media
coverage of aviator
Charles Lindbergh's
record-breaking
transatlantic flight in
the *Spirit of St. Louis*
(1925).

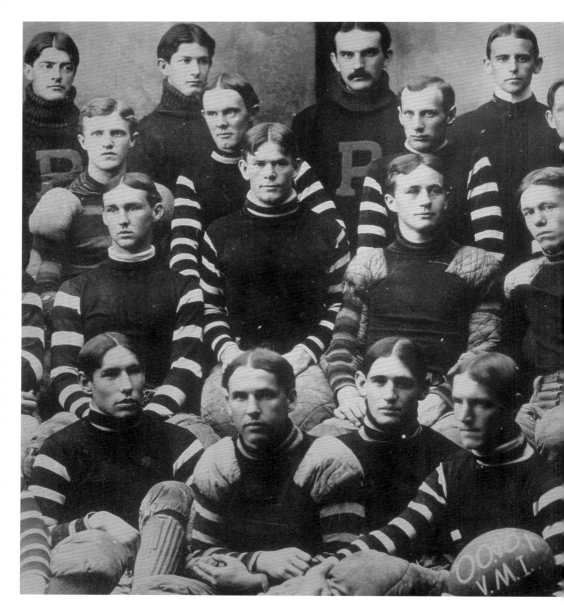

Left:
Probably the football
team of the Virginia
Military Institute,
wearing polo necks
with banded sleeves
in the team colours. The
extra shoulder and knee
padding worn by some
hints at the exaggerated
silhouette adopted later
in the century, while the
letter sweater became a
fashion staple (c. 1900).

Below:
Members of the
Canadian Silver Seven
ice-hockey team (now
the Ottawa Senators)
in full colour (1905).

Opposite:
Dizzy Dean of the
Chicago Cubs in
cropped trousers, a
short-sleeved T-shirt
over a vest and the
now ubiquitous baseball
cap (September 1938).

Left:
Captains of the
American and Canadian
third Winter Olympic
ice-hockey teams shake
hands at Lake Placid,
New York. Sweatshirts
and pants in knitted
jersey fabric are two
of the most significant
garments to have
made the transition
from sports to fashion
(February 1932).

Right:
The Household Brigade
cricket club. Sporting
blazers and flannels
would by the end of
World War I become
acceptable as informal
everyday wear (1912).

Below:
Oarsmen at Henley
Royal Regatta in blazers,
flannels and boaters
shading themselves
with parasols. Coloured
hatbands and braiding,
as well as the appropriate
tie, signified team
allegiance (1908).

Opposite left:
American Fashions in
The Sartorial Art Journal,
New York. Blazers
originated as part of
the naval uniform and
traditionally carried

brass or black buttons
with a crest or emblem,
such as an anchor.
Worn with white or
grey flannels they have
become a fashion staple
(June 1905).

Opposite right:
Film star John Gilbert
relaxes in a striped
blazer, white flannels
and white canvas or
buckskin shoes ('white
bucks' as they were
known in America),
all garments originally
worn for sport (1926).

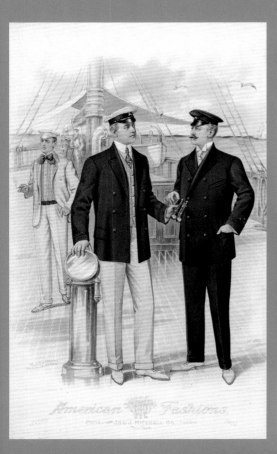

Right:
When the Prince of
Wales appeared on
the golf course at St
Andrew's in this outfit,
he ensured its transition
from functional to
fashionable dress
(c. 1922).

Below left:
American Fashions.
A Norfolk-style suit,
a lounge suit and
a knickerbocker suit,
worn with a variety
of neckwear and either
a soft flat-top hat or
tweed cap, show little
of the informality that
golf wear soon reached.
Lace-up half boots were
soon to be replaced by
brogues on the fairway
(June 1905).

Below right:
Knitwear had only
been worn by both
sexes for sports before
World War I. After
the war a craze for
knitting ensured that
Fair Isle sweaters, or
jazz jumpers, became
immensely popular
as fashion garments
(1920–30).

Opposite:
Esquire magazine.
Golf wear has remained
an arena in which men
can express a liking
for colour and pattern
(1936).

Left:
René Lacoste (middle right) and fellow members of the French Davis Cup team in V-neck sweaters and flannel trousers. Lacoste's blazer pocket carries his iconic crocodile logo, emblem of a now-global sportswear brand, which began with a cotton piqué knit shirt in 1927 (c. 1930).

Below:
American Fashions. Tennis played in a single- or double-breasted flannel suit is now hard to imagine (1905).

Below:
Global giant sportswear brand Nike kits out many top sportsmen, including Rafael Nadal, here winning Wimbledon. His clothes on court demonstrate the total integration of sportswear with street fashion today (2008).

Opposite:
Tennis champion Fred Perry invented the sweatband and launched a clothing range in the late 1940s. Fred Perry shirts became popular with youth subcultures, including mods and skinheads, later in the century (1934).

Right:
Captain Robert Falcon
Scott on skis in
Antarctica in a hooded
parka and trousers
specially made for him
by Burberry, whose
protective windproof
clothing and tents had
saved, it was claimed,
many a Polar explorer
from death by exposure
(1912).

Opposite:
German advertisement
for skiwear. A thick
white sweater, thigh-
high gaiters, a hat
and gloves, though
functional, are not
yet streamlined or
waterproof (1907).

Winter-Nummer

Illustrirte Zeitung

ERICH ERLER

Below:
Article in *Esquire*
magazine. This grey
gaberdine suit for skiing
accessorized with a
grey flannel plaid shirt,
Tyrolean pattern challis
tie, black felt Tyrolean
hat and 'peasant'
mittens would have
cut quite a dash on the
slopes. Gaberdine is a
semi-waterproof fabric,
owing to its twill
construction, but more
practical skiwear can
be seen on the figure
on the roof of the station
wagon (1937).

GABARDINE SKI SUIT *(January Esquire)* For most of their profits in ski merchandise, the
retail store must appeal to the novice, because there are more novices than experts thus far in this
country. This new double-breasted gabardine ski suit was introduced, and is favored by ski
meisters. The trousers are adapted for "down hill" skiing and are cut quite full and taper very
sharply into the tops of the boots. Heavy woolen hose are worn under the trousers.
Experts who ski on high slopes require the wind jacket, but even experts find the jacket of this
suit ideal for wear after skiing.
The lapels are convertible so that in a heavy wind they may be buttoned up for protection at the
neck and chest.
Accompanying this ski suit is a grey Glen Urquhart shirt of very light weight flannel and with it is
worn a green challis Tyrolean tie in peasant pattern. The hat is an authentic Austrian fashion from
the Tyrol, as are the peasant mittens. The ski boots are the correct model as worn by professionals
and experts both here and abroad.
Favored by all ski experts is the Norwegian Rucksack. It is made on a practical lightweight alu-
minum frame, so designed that it doesn't bounce against the back. It is arranged so that lunch, first
aid equipment, and other cross country equipment may be carried.

BLACK ROUGH-FINISHED FELT FOR
TYROLEAN HAT

GRAY GABARDINE SKI FABRIC

GRAY FLANNEL PLAID SHIRTING

TYROLEAN PATTERN CHALLIS TIE

Below:
Members of the British ski team wearing waterproof jackets, sweaters and stretch pants prepare for the Olympics in Switzerland (February 1936).

THE SUNAIRE ❧ THE SPEEDAIRE

combining them all in a fashion ruggedly masculine. Typically Jantzen in its permanent perfect fit, its seasonal style and color leadership, and in the truly marvelous elasticity of the Jantzen-stitch. It really is easier to swim in a Jantzen. ❧ In addition to the Sunaire and the Speedaire, (both illustrated), there are many other smart models for men, women and children...including the popular Shouldaire, men's and boys' Diving and Speed Suits, and Twosomes for men and women. You'll find the famous red Diving Girl emblem on every genuine Jantzen. Your weight is your size. ❧ Jantzen Knitting Mills, Portland, Oregon; Vancouver, Canada; London, England; Sydney, Australia.

Jantzen

The suit that changed bathing to swimming

JANTZEN KNITTING MILLS, (Dept. 104), Portland, Oregon
Please send me style folder in color featuring 1931 models.
Women's ☐   Men's ☐

Name _____

Address _____

Opposite:
Advertisement for Jantzen, which by 1930 was the market leader in swimwear. Their exclusive knitting process, Jantzen-stitch, gave a streamlined fit without sagging (September 1931).

Left above:
Advertisement for Jantzen, established in 1910. When Johnny Weissmuller of Tarzan fame appeared in trunks in 1929, the all-in-one swimsuit quickly went out of fashion (1936).

Left below:
Australian Olympic medallist Grant Hackett competes in a streamlined aerodynamic all-in-one suit made by his sponsors, Speedo, one of several Australian sports- and casualwear brands that include Quiksilver, O'Neill, Rip Curl and Mambo (2005).

Following spread:
Surfers on the beach in Sydney mostly wear an all-in-one style to protect themselves from board rash. Owing to its beach culture, Australia has since become one of the leading manufacturers in surf- and swimwear (c. 1935).

1900—1939
DRESSING DOWN, DRESSING UP

Below:
Since the seventeenth century the dressing gown has been worn by men relaxing at home. Artist William Nicholson wears a spotted silk one over his shirt and trousers (1912).

Opposite:
Advertisement for Cooper's-Bennington all-in-one 'spring needle knit' combinations. The Cooper's mill at Kenosha, Wisconsin, developed the Kenosha Klosed Krotch, a diagonal access opening at the back of the combinations (1919).

Sleeved cotton or woollen vests and long johns, essential winter wear in the days before central heating or thermal fibres, have long disappeared. As housing was modernized, more active lifestyles pursued and textile technology improved, underwear got lighter, leaner and more comfortable. In 1934, when Clark Gable stripped off his shirt in *It Happened One Night* to reveal his naked chest, the attraction for wearing a vest was questioned. However, two later screen idols, Marlon Brando and James Dean, were to transform the short-sleeved cotton T-shirt, army-issue underwear worn by GIs during World War II, into a perennial fashion item. Underwear is now often visibly on display, from the elastic waistband of a pair of Calvin Kleins to the string tank vest.

Conversely, the dressing gown has hardly changed at all. For centuries it has held a special place in the male wardrobe, originating in the late seventeenth century as a T-shaped robe to wear at home, often made of exotic oriental fabrics instead of the elaborate, stiff, heavy coat that was fashionable at the time. During the eighteenth century, men were spotted wearing dressing gowns in coffee houses and many were even depicted wearing them in portraits. By the twentieth century, however, they were entirely reserved for domestic and private spaces, which is perhaps why they are often extravagantly patterned colourful statements of luxury and excess.

If men were able to express in private their inner dandy through the dressing gown, they could publicly portray an alternative image through fancy dress. Costume balls, fancy dress 'routs' and entertainments at country-house weekends were extremely popular in the interwar period. Of course, costume is not the same as fashion, but the two met somewhere in the middle with high camp. The gay community was necessarily at this time underground – coded messages were invested in dress, a secret language that would not be articulated until well into the second half of the century: for the time being, literally and metaphorically, kept in the closet.

Buy Cooper's-Bennington Spring Needle Underwear. It has that all-over elasticity which comes from spring needle knitting and gives perfect-fitting comfort. Be sure that the word "Bennington" is on the garment label.

COOPER'S
BENNINGTON

Spring Needle Underwear

For the sake of added elasticity—the stretch that springs back—all good underwear has spring needle cuffs and ankles. But Cooper's-Bennington is spring needle knit throughout. Dealers have your size in many weights, styles and prices.

Makers also of Black Cat Reinforced Hosiery for men, women and children

BLACK CAT TEXTILES COMPANY
HOME OFFICE: KENOSHA, WISCONSIN

Factories at Kenosha and Sheboygan, Wis., Harvard, Ill., and Bennington, Vt.

Below left:
French advertisement
for Dr Robertson's
Lotion. The private
nature of the dressing
gown allowed for
extrovert patterned
fabrics to be used – in
the seventeenth century
rich oriental brocades
and 'bizarre' silks, here
brightly coloured art
deco-style motifs (1924).

Below right:
The epitome of urbane
elegance, Noel Coward,
English actor and
playwright, in costume
for *Tonight At 8.30* at
the Phoenix Theatre,
London, wearing a
spotted silk dressing
gown and matching
cravat (1936).

Opposite:
The cover of *Man and
his Clothes*, published
by Fairchild, features
a dapper dandy in a
striped satin dressing
gown (May 1936).

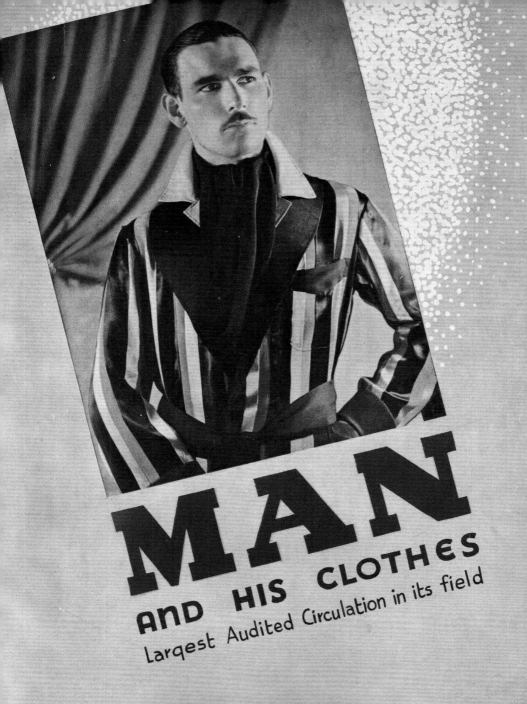

MAN
AND HIS CLOTHES
Largest Audited Circulation in its field

ONE SHILLING   MAY 1936

Opposite:
'Teddy' in a lamé
tailcoat and wide
trousers with a silk
high-collared blouse
and hair styled by
Antoine. At a time
when homosexuality
was illegal, high
camp, such as this
outfit, was reserved
for private occasions
or for performance
(1932).

Left:
Cecil Beaton in
eighteenth-century
costume. Photographer
and author of diaries
and several books
on fashion, Beaton
considered himself an
authority on dress and
won an Oscar for his
costume designs for
George Cukor's *My Fair
Lady* in 1964 (c. 1935).

194

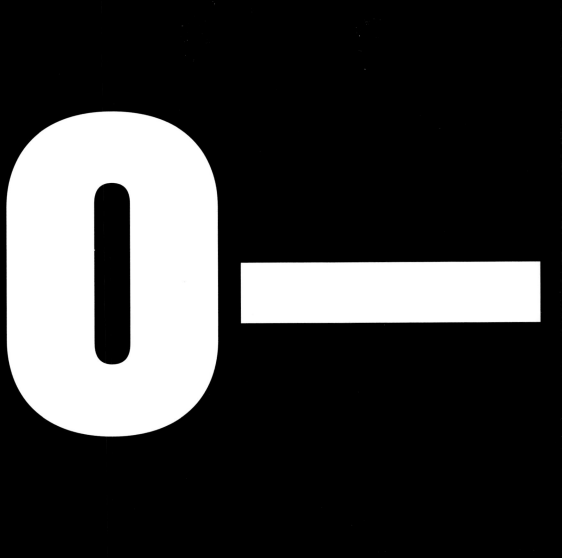

1940—
REBEL

Below:
After the Occupation
by the Nazis in 1940,
anti-Fascist groups in
Paris took to wearing
the yellow star as an
emblem of protest and
in support of the Jews
(c. 1941).

Opposite:
Cover of *Notre Combat*,
a French weekly.
Zazous were addicted
to American swing
music, which originated
in Harlem; soon the
craze swept through
Europe thanks to the
success of musicians
such as Cab Calloway
and Benny Goodman.
The term 'Zazou' may
have originated from
a song by Calloway
(May 1943).

So-called subcultures and their associated sartorial modes are not a new phenomenon. Artistic garb is a form of subcultural dress, and gangs of hoodlums and hooligans operating on the streets from New York to Manchester at the turn of the twentieth century declared their allegiances by wearing specific items of dress. The classification of the adolescent by sociologists early in the twentieth century (and the subsequent coining of the term 'teenager') established the perception of the young as a separate species, often at odds with a dominant culture that regarded them with anxiety and suspicion. Far from being dampened by outrage, the dress adopted by subcultures within this youth sector became a tool of defiance and political resistance, emerging as one of the most significant influences on fashion in the second half of the twentieth century.

Subcultural dress and music went hand in hand. The hot jazz and swing music that accompanied the Harlem Renaissance of the 1920s established distinctive styles among its followers. Jazzmen and fans favoured an exaggerated dressed-up look: the word 'zoot' was a term of approval that by the late 1930s described the suit that, with its extreme padded shoulders, peaked lapels, extra long jacket and voluminous peg-top trousers with narrow ankles, had become the sartorial badge of young urban African-American and Hispanic hipsters.

The zoot suiters achieved notoriety by flaunting their swagger and defying clothes rationing regulations after 1941, an act considered unpatriotic and one of the factors that contributed to the Zoot Suit Riots in California in 1943. In Los Angeles gangs of off-duty marines set upon the zoot-suited *pachucos* (slang for Mexican-American youth gangs) and, despite not being the perpetrators of the ensuing violence, many zoot suiters were arrested and jailed.

Similar treatment of the zoot suiters' French counterparts, the Zazous, took place during the Occupation in Paris, where swing music was immensely popular but banned by the Nazi regime. Harsh punishments were meted out to the Zazous, though not as harsh as those imposed on members of the underground 'Swing' youth groups in Germany, who refused to join the Hitler Youth and defied the regime by adopting unkempt clothing and growing their hair long.

Teenage rebellion after World War II continued to be a matter of concern for conventional society, reflected in such films as *The Wild One* and *Rebel Without a Cause* in the early 1950s. The succession of subcultural groups, such as the Teddy boys, bikers, beats, beatniks, folkies, hipsters, modernists and Left Bank existentialists, all invariably associated with a particular genre of music and, identifying themselves through a particular style of dress, represented the rejection of the older generation's social and cultural norms by a booming and increasingly affluent teenage population. This tactic of subversion through dress was to become increasingly influential in the postwar years, although the numbers that actually wore such styles should not be overestimated, and one is naturally wary of such rigid classifications. Of these minority groups, it was the modernists who most directly influenced menswear from the late 1940s onwards. The sharp minimalism of cool bebop hipsters and modernist jazzmen, after whom the mods (as they became known) were named, launched a new look, harbinger of the peacock revolution that followed in the 1960s.

More than anything, the use of clothing to express rebellion paved the way for the acceptance of difference in dress, contributing to the fragmentation of fashion and culture of indifference towards dress that we recognize today. By their nature, subcultures are minority groups: most teenagers (by the early 1950s in America constituting a major section of the consumer market) were fairly conventional and subcultures such as the beats impacted very little, if at all, on the mass market and the clean-cut Ivy League college-boy look of sports jacket, Brooks Brothers shirt, chinos, white socks, penny loafers and short hair (not much different from the older generation's style). Even Elvis, hero of a generation, gave up the rebel image he cultivated at the start of his career, instead donning more and more lavish costumes such as jewelled cloaks and high-collared jumpsuits.

3ᵉ Année. (Nlle série). - N° 46.   **TOUS LES 3ᶠ SAMEDIS**   22 Mai 1943.

NOTRE COMBAT

HEBDOMADAIRE POLITIQUE LITTÉRAIRE SATIRIQUE

DEUX GÉNÉRATIONS

— *Nous, au moins, nous prenions des bois, des collines. Ceux-là ne savent plus prendre que le maquis !...*

PUBLIÉ A PARIS POUR TOUTE LA FRANCE

Opposite:
In France, the Zazous
expressed their
opposition to the
Nazi regime through
their dress. This
Zazou typifies the
style: massive shades,
slicked-back hair 'oiled
like a salad', pencil-thin
moustache, white socks
and thick-soled shoes
(1944).

Left above:
Zoot suiters celebrated
a subversive dandyism,
'a solid set of threads'.
Despite being quashed
by the authorities,
both the Zazous and
zoot suiters prepared
the ground for the
revolution in men's
fashion after World
War II, and the look
has been revisited
ever since (1942).

Left below:
Jerome Mendelson
models a zoot suit: a
long oversized draped
jacket, high peg-top
trousers with narrow
cuffs at the ankle,
a flamboyant tie and
an elongated dog chain
suspended from the
waist (1942).

148

1940–
Rebel

Right above:
John Hazel, Harold Wilmot and John Richards arrive at Tilbury docks from the Caribbean on the ex-troop ship *Empire Windrush*. Their smartly tailored clothes show the influence of zoot suits and the more 'dressed-up' style of black culture (1948).

Right below:
The Will Mastin Trio. Sammy Davis Jr (centre) wears a checked zoot suit, large bow tie and wide-brimmed white fedora (c. 1945).

Opposite:
Malcolm X, Black Power activist, wearing his signature Clubmaster Ray-Bans. In the 1940s he wore a sky-blue zoot suit, a style he swapped for a more sober look as he sought political and religious respectability (early 1960s).

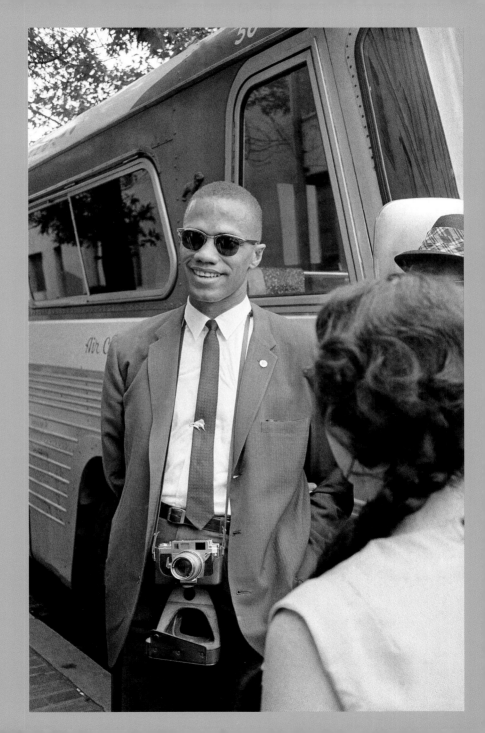

Below left:
Down Beat magazine.
Dizzy Gillespie, sharp-
suited hipster and
king of bebop, wears
his trademark beret,
horn-rimmed glasses
and goatee beard
(May 1947).

Below right:
Modernists and hipsters
at a Dizzy Gillespie
concert in California.
Bebop musicians and
their fans adopted a
pared-down aesthetic
that can be seen in
the collarless jacket
on the left. Shades,
berets and flamboyant
ties were essential
accessories (1948).

Opposite:
Frank Sinatra, idol of
the teenage American
bobby-soxers, who
began his career with
Benny Goodman and
Slim Gaillard, prepares
to sing with the New
York Philharmonic
Orchestra. His draped
pants, spectator shoes,
stylish short-sleeved
shirt and quiffed hair
show the influence
of the zoot/swing style
(1943).

Right above:
Collarless jackets and
spotted scarf ties next
to uniforms at Bop City
opening night in New
York (1949).

Right below:
Cool cat Miles Davis,
regarded by many in the
1960s as the epitome of
the hipster, portrayed in
Gap's 1990s advertising
campaign for khaki
pants, a lightweight
smart/casual trouser
that, like chinos,
originally derived from
military wear (1960s).

Opposite:
A teenager from Des
Moines, Iowa, in a letter
cardigan, white T-shirt
and buckled western
belt sports a flat-top
haircut. As reflected
in films such as *Rebel
Without a Cause* (1955),
postwar American
society felt threatened
by its mushrooming
adolescent population
(1944).

Miles Davis wore khakis.

GAP
KHAKIS

Andy Warhol wore khakis.

GAP
KHAKIS

BASS AMERICA

IN A COUNTRY FAMOUS FOR PASSING FASHIONS,
TRUE CLASSICS ARE REVERED.

Fifty-eight years ago in the tiny town of Wilton, Maine,
G. H. Bass & Co. introduced a men's shoe that was
to become the essence of classic American styling.

The Weejun.® First a hit on college
campuses, the Weejun has been worn
by movie stars and presidents. The
most-read daily newspaper in the U.S.
called the Weejun "In for Infinity." People

become so attached to their Weejuns that they will re-sole
favorite pairs over and over again. Besides its timeless
styling, the Weejun has the incomparable feel of a hand
sewn leather upper. Loyal wearers say it creates a sense of
familiarity between foot and shoe that simply cannot be
duplicated. The Bass Weejun. After fifty-eight years, it's not
just a shoe. It's a legend.

*The Bass® Weejun features a full grain leather upper that is sewn by hand in the United States.
For more information contact Justin Morgan, P.O. Box 19,
Melton Mowbray, Leicestershire, LE13 OKX Phone and Fax 0664-62476.*

"TO BUILD THE BEST POSSIBLE
SHOE FOR THE PURPOSE
FOR WHICH IT WILL BE USED."
George Henry Bass, 1876

Bass®

THE LOOK THAT NEVER WEARS OUT™

155

1940–
Rebel

Opposite:
A college student
in a single-breasted
jacket, ankle-grazing
grey flannels and
loafers: classic Ivy
League style, so-called
because it originated
on the East Coast
campuses (c. 1950).

Left above:
Gap's advertising
campaign for khakis
featured cultural icons
such as Kerouac, Davis
and, here, Andy Warhol
before he went pop,
underlining the power
of the historic image
on fashion (late 1950s).

Left below:
Slip-on loafers, derived
from early North
American moccasins,
became the key
footwear of the Ivy
Leaguers in the 1950s,
Bass Weejuns (from
Norwegian moccasins)
being one of the most
popular brands. It was
fashionable to tuck
a good-luck penny in
the vamp welt, giving
rise to the term penny
loafers (1950s).

Right above:
Artist John Minton
in turned-up jeans,
striped casual shirt and
T-shirt. The influence
of American music
and film made jeans
fashionable among
teenagers, especially
art students. In Britain,
Lee Cooper had been
manufacturing jeans
as casual rather than
utilitarian wear since
1946; Levi's were
virtually unobtainable
in Britain until the late
1950s (1951).

Right below:
Young men in baseball
jackets and peg-top
trousers gaze into the
window of Williams
& Co. in Charing Cross
Road, London, the
centre of American
clothing imports since
East End tailor Cecil
Gee launched his
'American Look' suits
in 1946, to the joy of
those used to khakis
and demob outfits
(1951).

Opposite:
Australian Jack Perry
outside Lord's Cricket
Ground in jeans,
belted leather jacket
and baseball boots.
His clothes, long hair
and beard give him a
decidedly beatnik look
that must have seemed
exotic to Londoners still
in the grip of postwar
austerity (1953).

Opposite:
James Dean in jeans on the set of *Rebel Without a Cause*, the seminal teenage angst movie (1955).

Left:
Marlon Brando's muscular physique was set off to perfection in his role in Tennessee Williams's *A Streetcar Named Desire* (1947) in which he appeared either topless or in a tight, torn, sweat-stained T-shirt. He started a craze for which he claimed he could have earned more money than as an actor (c. 1951).

372·639

Opposite:
Marlon Brando as
gang leader Johnny
Strabler in *The Wild
One*, wearing the Schott
Brothers of New York
Perfecto leather jacket,
based on a World War
II model. The jacket
came to express the
tough-guy image of
a generation of bikers,
greasers, ton-up boys
and Hell's Angels
and has become a cult
collectors' garment
(1953).

Left:
Bikers, including the
Reverend Bill Shergold
(distinguished by his
dog collar), outside
the Ace Café in North
London wearing
studded leathers, jeans
and peaked caps (1962).

Right above:
Drainpipe leather
trousers and winkle-
picker boots with a
quiff: a fusion of Elvis,
rocker, 1960s and punk
styles in Japan (c. 1984).

Right below:
Yoyogi Park in Tokyo
is a favourite arena for
display and spectacle
among youth groups
in Japan. The Japanese
have absorbed much
of the music and fashion
of Western European
subcultures. Here, a
group of boys parade
in rocker gear (c. 1984).

Opposite:
Elements of biker
gear combined with
fetish wear have
been adopted as the
signature look of the
butch gay community,
as can be seen here
at the annual Gay
Carnival in Hollywood,
California (1982).

805

Opposite:
Elvis in a zoot-style
suit, black shirt, tie and
loafers, combining overt
sexuality with disparate
elements from various
styles to create his early
rebel persona (1956).

Left:
Elvis became the
musical and sartorial
icon of a generation
of fans the world over,
but his increasingly
extravagant stage
wear, which included
a gold lamé and
rhinestone-encrusted
tuxedo costing $10,000,
positioned him firmly
in the mainstream
of popular culture.
It is his earlier edgy
look that retains its
perennial appeal (1956).

Right:
The film *Blue Hawaii*.
As he toned down
his image to appeal
to a wider audience,
Elvis wore clothes that
were more mainstream.
Hawaiian shirts were
popularized by surfers
in the late 1940s and
remain part of the
scene today. They were
given a modern twist
by Australian brand
Mambo in the 1990s
(1961).

Below:
New Yorker Eliot
Hubbard with some of
his vintage Hawaiian
shirt collection (1985).

Opposite:
An authentic
representation of cowboy
gear by photographer
Kurt Markus. Tattered
jeans contrast with an
immaculate white shirt
with an appliqué key-
pattern frilled detail and
a Stetson (date unknown).

Left above:
Multimedia star Gene
Autry, known as the
'Singing Cowboy',
wears a western shirt
lavishly embroidered
with roses and whose
cuffs are outlined
with decorative piping.
The rise of country
and western music
in tandem with the
arrival of television
popularized the cowboy
style. Autry's 'Tom
Mix' hat calls to mind
the Hollywood actor
who defined the western
genre (1946).

Left below:
An advertisement for
Stetson cologne. Matthew
McConaughey evokes
the rugged appeal of the
cowboy (2004).

Right:
Dandy Bunny Roger
was one of a select
group of men in
the early 1950s who
adopted the Edwardian
cut as defined by Savile
Row tailoring. He is
seen here in a tightly
waisted overcoat,
bowler and highly
polished boots. The
look (and the name)
was translated into
a new style by the
Teddy boys (1954).

Opposite:
Teddy boys in long
draped jackets,
waistcoats with watch
chains, peg-top trousers
and bootlace ties.
Mainly from working-
class backgrounds, the
Teddy boys subverted
the dress of their so-
called superiors (1954).

Below:
A queue for Mr Rose,
the barber who claimed
to have invented the
quiff, the Teddy boys'
signature haircut. The
quiff was accompanied
by a 'd.a.' (duck's arse),
a point of hair at the
back of the neck. An
essential accessory was
a comb kept in the back
pocket. Advertisements
for perms and manicures
hint at the growing
importance of grooming
for the new dandy
(November 1954).

Opposite:
Products like Brylcreem
were essential for
achieving the correct
hairstyle for Teddy
boys, as well as for the
more conservative man
(1954).

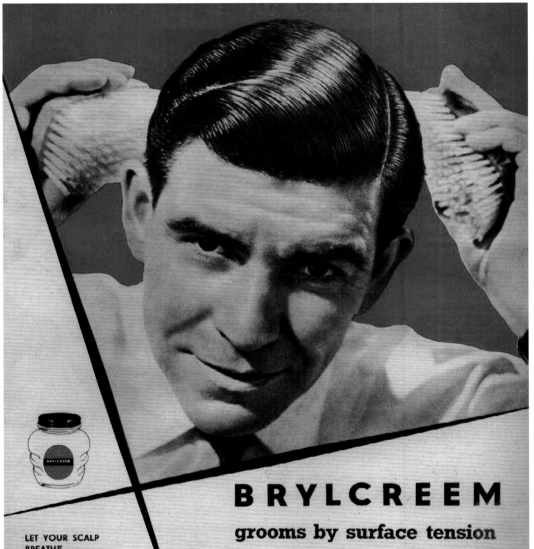

BRYLCREEM

grooms by surface tension

Any liquid always strives to reduce its surface area when in contact with air . . . this is known as **Surface Tension** —and it is the basis on which Brylcreem works. A thin film of Brylcreem oil, together with a bland aqueous solution, coats every hair-strand and the surface tension holds the hairs together firmly but gently. Every hair is supple; every hair is lustrous. Avoid that greasy, over-oily look. Use Brylcreem, the healthy hairdressing, for the clean, smart look.

for smart, healthy hair

LET YOUR SCALP BREATHE . . . ENCOURAGE YOUR HAIR TO LIVE

In keeping your hair and scalp healthy, Brylcreem's surface film of oil acts as a filter, which prevents micro-organisms from reaching down into the scalp. Massage with Brylcreem also frees the mouths of the follicles along which the hair grows, thus facilitating the normal flow of sebum, the scalp's natural oil. As a result, the hair is kept free from dandruff and dryness and the scalp has a chance to breathe—vitally important to the growth of strong, healthy hair. Ask for Brylcreem, the *healthy* hairdressing, in tubs 1/6, 2/3 and 4/1, or handy tubes 2/6.

Right:
Ancestors of the
hippies, beats wore
chinos, scruffy
sweaters, work shirts
and army surplus. Here,
a beat in flip-flops and
tattered jeans waits for
a performance licence
in Los Angeles. By
the late 1950s the term
'beatnik' was coined
to describe a younger
generation that adopted
polo necks, sandals
and black, black, black
(August 1959).

Opposite:
Cover for Jack
Kerouac's seminal
beat novel *On the Road*,
showing the author
and Neal Cassady
demonstrating typical
beat style, defined by
Kerouac as 'worn out
and sad'. Their studied
indifference to fashion
expressed disdain for
conventional society.
The beats loved bebop,
abstract expressionist
art and existentialist
philosophy (1955).

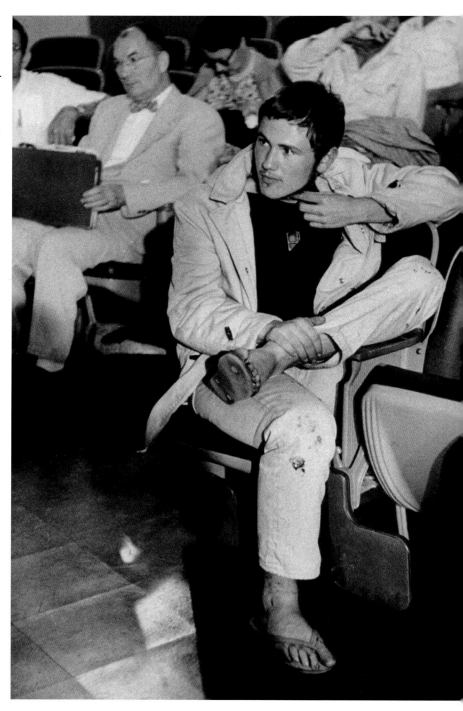

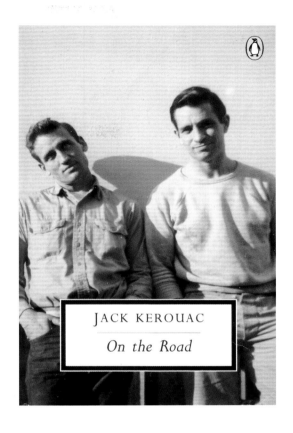

JACK KEROUAC

On the Road

Right:
CND protestors at
Aldermaston, UK,
in rain-soaked duffel
coats, macs and
anoraks. Politics and
protest combined with
anti-vanity and anti-
fashion (April 1958).

Below:
An advertisement
for duffel coats:
warm, practical and
perennially popular
(1980s).

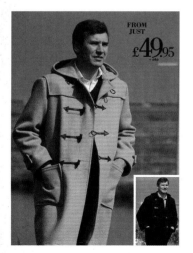

FROM
JUST
£49.95
+ p&p

1940—
PEACOCK

Below:
Colourful ties by Emilio Pucci in Italy foreshadow the swirling psychedelic prints of the later 1960s (1960).

Opposite:
Customized second-hand army surplus, ethnic braid, beads, tinted glasses, bare feet and a glorious red Afro sum up the hippie look (1969).

Postwar austerity in Europe was, by the mid 1950s, beginning to be replaced by a new silhouette, as well as by increasing use of colour and pattern, a fundamental shift in menswear that would explode into the so-called 'peacock revolution' of the 1960s. Italian tailors such as Brioni introduced the 'Continental look', a leaner, sharper cut launched through fashion shows and shops on both sides of the Atlantic and worn by the stars of the burgeoning film industry based at the Cinecittà studios in Rome.

Savile Row, still the bastion of traditional bespoke, was slow to respond to the new look and, ironically, it was Hardy Amies, a women's couturier, who initiated change. In 1959 he launched a line of modern ready-to-wear suits for tailoring chain Hepworth's. Acknowledging the influence of *la bella figura* Italian style, Amies introduced suits with vents in the back, lower-waisted jackets with two buttons and a more fitted line, a look he successfully exported to America. By the early 1960s, Paris-based couturier Pierre Cardin had become an influential force whose futuristic collections would later combine mod style with a space-age aesthetic. In 1960 he launched a collarless jacket that became the template for the early Beatles look. However, it was a new generation of London-based entrepreneurs that turned around the world of men's fashion by addressing the demands of the young urban male consumer, who now wanted to dress differently

from his father in up-to-the-minute styles sold in modern retail environments that responded quickly to new trends. It was John Stephen, known as The King of Carnaby Street, who was the driving force behind this liberation.

Stephen started his career working at Vince, a shop in Soho that imported Italian separates and jeans from Paris. Opening his first premises in Carnaby Street in 1957, he soon owned numerous outlets in and around London, kick-starting the proliferation of boutiques that made London synonymous with the swinging scene. Materials such as corduroy, satin and velvet were made into suits and hipster trousers in bold hues. Flowered shirts, colourful ties and cord 'Beatle caps' completed the London look, soon exported across the Atlantic by way of pop groups, models and designers whose clothes were manufactured there under licence in profitable tie-ups with American garment manufacturers.

In 1966 *Time* magazine's article on 'Swinging London' included a map of fashionable hot spots for the in-crowd and trendy boutiques in Carnaby Street as well as the more exclusive King's Road. Expensive outfitters, such as Mr Fish in Piccadilly, and elite tailoring firms, such as Blades in Dover Street, catered for the new pop aristocracy, kitting them out as dandyish Regency bucks in fitted double-breasted suits, high collars and frilled shirts – specializing in what Andy Warhol nicknamed the 'Pakistani-Indian-international-jet-set-hippie-look'. Savile Row received a further boost when Tommy Nutter opened his premises in 1969. His trademark suits with a tight jacket, wide lapels edged with his signature contrasting braid and flared trousers, all cut in a medley of pattern, appealed to both sexes, and his clients included Mick and Bianca Jagger, Twiggy and The Beatles.

For the trendsetters and beautiful people, the commercialism of Carnaby Street and the cliché of Swinging London soon became a turn-off. By the second half of the 1960s many were involved in the psychedelic drug counterculture that originated, along with its accompanying alternative lifestyle, on the West Coast of America. Here, the hippies eschewed mainstream fashion for an eclectic mixture of ethnic, exotic, home-made and second-hand vintage clothing in their search for Utopia. Men wore ethnic jewelry, picked up on the Eastern hippie trail or in a boutique in Haight-Ashbury in San Francisco, and grew their hair, the longer, the better; many also adopted droopy moustaches, a fashion that went on well into the 1970s. By the late 1960s the hedonistic idealism of the younger generation was giving way to disillusion in the wake of the Vietnam War, student protest and looming economic crisis. The hippie style, like the mod style before it, became the victim of commercialism as it was appropriated by the dominant culture. However, its ethos of dressing up and ostentatious androgyny would continue as high camp in the shape of glam-rock stars David Bowie and Marc Bolan during the 1970s.

Below:
Italian tailoring was admired for its stylish cut: short straight single-breasted jackets and tapered trousers without turn-ups created *la bella figura* silhouette of the Continental style, displayed here at the annual San Remo show. The craft-based manufacture of many Italian goods, especially shoes and leather accessories, is still highly valued today (September 1958).

Opposite:
GQ (*Gentlemen's Quarterly*). Leon Kuzmanoff's striking illustration for the November 1960 cover features a man in a tangerine dinner jacket by After Six looking at a burst of fireworks. Launched in 1957, originally as *Apparel Arts*, the magazine was taken over by Condé Nast in 1983, since when it has successfully targeted the young metrosexual with an upmarket mix of fashion, style and culture (1960).

THE FASHION MAGAZINE FOR MEN

GQ

GENTLEMEN'S QUARTERLY

NOVEMBER 1960 ONE DOLLAR

Stritzel
TWEED

"Sous-bois", création de **PIERRE CARDIN** 118, Fg-St-Honoré, Paris, éditée par BRIL
STRITZEL-TWEED, 26, rue de la Pépinière - Paris 8e

Opposite:
Advertisement for
Pierre Cardin in *Adam*.
Through licensing
deals, as here with
garment-manufacturer
Bril, his ready-to-
wear clothing became
relatively affordable and
his slim, tubular line
immensely influential.
The jacket with a fly
front and stand collar
is a prototype for the
Nehru jacket (December
1961).

Left:
Pioneering couturier
Pierre Cardin launched
his first menswear line
at the Crillon Hotel in
Paris. Using students
as models, he showed
collarless jackets in
corduroy and cotton
(1960).

Right:
Early in The Beatles'
meteoric career their
stage wear was made
by Soho tailor Dougie
Millings. John Lennon
wears a collarless jacket
that refers back to the
modernists via Cardin,
and sports the 'Beatle'
haircut that became the
signature look for the
younger generation in
the early 1960s (1963).

Opposite above:
'Cosmos' suit at
the Victoria & Albert
Museum, London.
Along with other young
Parisian designers,
Cardin explored
futuristic concepts
inspired by the space
race. Suits were
abandoned for sweaters,
sleeveless jerkins
fastened with zips and
jersey trousers. Many
of his designs were
intended to be unisex
(1967).

Opposite below:
Despite being too
radical for many, this
Australian white suit
jacket with front zip
fastening, stand collar
and epaulettes reflects
the widespread
influence of Cardin
by the end of the 1960s
(c. 1969).

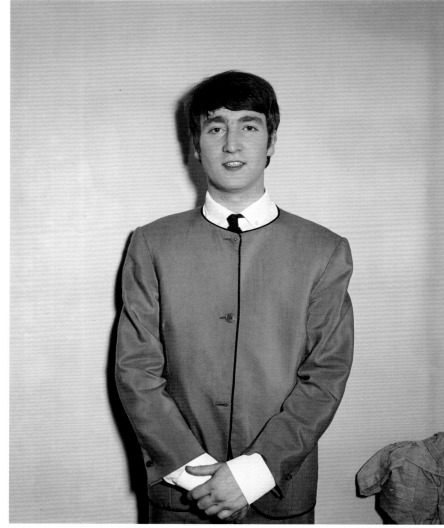

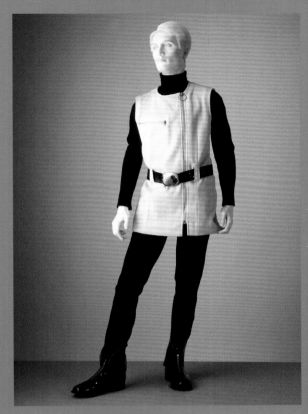

Right:
The magazine *Adam* advertises a paisley-patterned silk foulard jacket by Christian Dior Boutique that was designed to be worn at Cannes and Monte Carlo (June/July 1961).

Below:
Hardy Amies brought in new wave ideas for menswear. Like Cardin, he broke the rules of tailoring, giving it a modern aesthetic with extrovert touches like the evening cape and fur duffel coat (September 1964).

Opposite:
Tim Glazier, scion of long-established London hatters Herbert Johnson, models a pink raw-silk trilby with a high crown and furled brim. During the 1960s, the firm was largely responsible for re-establishing hats as fashion items for men (1965).

190

1940–
Peacock

Below left:
Composer Sir Peter
Maxwell Davies in an
elephant-cord suit, polo
neck and Beatle boots
– an elastic gusseted
Chelsea boot with
a Cuban heel (early
1960s).

Below right:
Andy Warhol in black
and white; obsessed by
footwear, he regarded
Beatle boots as things
of beauty (1965).

Below:
Anello & Davide, a
theatrical footwear
company in London's
Covent Garden,
designed the Beatle
boot for The Beatles.
The boot became a
fashion icon for the
mods. Heels on men's
shoes rose in height
until the mid 1970s
(1965).

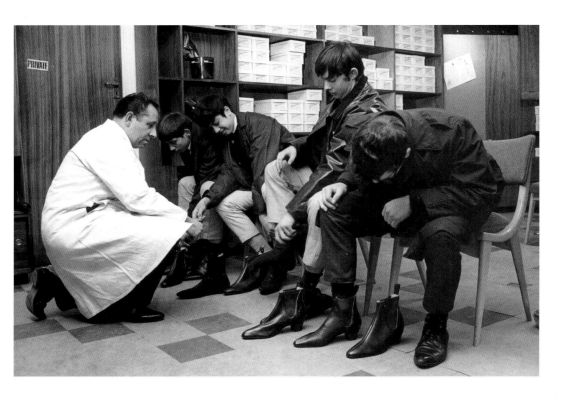

Below:
John Stephen (middle
right) launched His
Clothes in 1957 and by
1963 owned 18 shops
in Carnaby Street and
beyond. Catering to
the teenage market with
fast-changing stock and
outlets like amusement
arcades with blaring
music and staffed
by youthful assistants,
he transformed the
shopping experience
in Britain (1966).

Below:
Advertisement for Vince,
featuring Sean Connery
in jeans, espadrilles and
a denim striped Capri
shirt. Bill Green of Vince
imported Continental
casual clothes, including
hard-to-get Levi's, tight
sweaters and hipster
pants in flamboyant
colours and unusual
fabrics (early 1960s).

contemporary design in leisure wear

Vince

CAPRI SHIRT
No. 622 Typical of our exclusive styling in Navy/
White striped DENIM. Cut on generous lines and tapering
to waist.
Please state chest size. Add 1/- post and packing. **47/6**

Vince

EXCLUSIVE JEANS
No. 306 French style in "Faded" Blue DENIM
with 2 front and 2 hip pockets. **38/6**

No. 307 Tailored in DRILL with 2 front and 2 hip
pockets. IN BLACK OR THE NEW RIVIERA COLOUR,
SKY BLUE. **42/-**

Please state waist and inside leg measurements. All Jeans taper to 16in. Add 1s. 8d. post and packing.
24-page illustrated catalogue will be sent on request.

vince man's shop

15 Newburgh Street, Foubert's Place, Regent Street, London, W.1. GER 3730
Open Mon. Tues. Wed. Fri. 9 to 5.30 p.m. Thurs. 9 to 7 p.m. Sat. 9 to 3 p.m.
Vince Leisure Wear also on sale at James Grose Ltd. 379 Euston Road, N.W.1, and at Marshall & Snelgrove at Leeds, Manchester and Leicester

Right:
Jeff Beck of The
Yardbirds models
a flowered shirt by
John Stephen, who
successfully liberated
men's fashion and
paved the way for a less
gender-based approach
to dressing (1966).

Opposite:
Advertisement for
Harvey of Carnaby
Street's Tiles collection
at Jayson of New York.
British designers made
lucrative tie-ups with
American manufacturers
and outlets in the 1960s,
thereby disseminating
the London Look (1960s).

THE MOD SHIRTS ARE HERE

Mod ties and Mod sweaters too! That master Mod, Harvey of Carnaby Street, is behind it all. He's bringing the authentic Mod look from England exclusively to Jayson's new Tiles collection. There are shirts in bright, bold patterns and colors, with collar styles that'll really grab you. There are great new ties coordinated with the shirts. And there are turtleneck sweaters to top off the modern look of Mod. How's that for stirring up a revolution!

TilesT.M. **Collection by Harvey of Carnaby Street, designed exclusively for Jayson.** Harvey, captain of the Mod crew, wears a pink, high roll button down shirt, about $9. The cranberry shirt has a rounded point collar, about $7. The navy shirt has a high roll, spear point collar, about $7. The striped high turtleneck in 100% virgin worsted wool is about $25. The solid color sweater in 100% Shetland wool is about $11. Ties about $3 to $5. Prices slightly higher in the West. Jayson®, Inc., 390 Fifth Ave., N. Y. 10018. **Jayson**

Previous spread:
Models, including Ossie
Clark (middle left), pose
in front of Albert Little's
art nouveau-style
backdrop inside the
expensive Hung On
You Boutique in Cale
Street, Chelsea. Owned
by Michael Rainey,
it attracted a more
exclusive clientele than
Carnaby Street (1966).

Below left:
If Christopher Gibbs
represented the old
aristocracy, then David
Bailey represented the
new. Photographers,
actors, designers and
pop stars from working-
class backgrounds
began to make their
mark in what would be
called the 'youthquake'
of the 1960s (mid 1960s).

Below right:
Christopher Gibbs,
noted dandy and
aesthete, wears a white
lace shirt and dashing
hat in a pub. Younger
than the original
'Chelsea set' in the
late 1950s, he bridged
the gap into the 1960s,
mingling with the new
pop aristocracy (1966).

Opposite:
Mick Jagger in a
Grenadier uniform
jacket. Like Elvis's,
Jagger's image
was overtly sexual;
combining camp
with feminine agility,
he blurred gender
stereotypes (1967).

Far left:
Outside I Was Lord
Kitchener's Valet, a
boutique on London's
Portobello Road
specializing in vintage
military uniforms and
Victoriana (1967).

Left:
Jimi Hendrix epitomized
the rock/hippie style
with a fusion of ethnic
embroidery, skintight
velvet pants, scarves
and jewelry, topped
with an Afro hairstyle
(c. 1967).

Below:
Paul McCartney in
Cornwall while filming
*The Magical Mystery
Tour.* He wears an
Indian embroidered
shirt with a crochet
waistcoat and flared
trousers in typical
hippie bricolage style.
The Beatles' meeting
with the Maharishi
in the same year, and
subsequent trip to his
ashram, influenced
millions of fans
(September 1967).

Opposite:
The generation gap
demonstrated on
the streets of Sydney.
What looks like an
Indian tablecloth
has been turned into
a caftan (c. 1970).

Opposite:
Aristocratic trendsetters
Julian and Victoria
Ormsby-Gore swap
jackets, while interior
designer David Mlinaric
poses atop a Rolls
Royce in a rainy London
street (1968).

Far left:
Society photographer
Lord Patrick Litchfield,
every inch the Regency
buck, in a lavish
embroidered dinner
coat with lace jabot
at the neck (1968).

Left above:
At the memorial concert
for Brian Jones in Hyde
Park, Mick Jagger
wears a feminine white
shirt dress designed
by Michael Fish (1969).

Left below:
Mlinaric's striped
double-breasted
velvet suit made from
furnishing fabric was
designed by Michael
Fish, who had dragged
august Jermyn Street
shirtmaker Turnbull
& Asser into the modern
age by designing a
range of fantasy shirts.
In 1966 Fish set up
his own premises in
London's Piccadilly
specializing in shirts,
kipper ties and
successfully translating
hippie style into high-
end fashion (1968).

Right:
A model wearing
suits by Blades, an
exclusive Savile Row
tailor started in 1962
by gentleman amateur
Rupert Lycett Green
and East Ender Eric
Joy. Having initially
regarded the new
breed of tailors with
suspicion, if not outright
derision, 'old' Savile
Row began to recognize
the threat posed
by these newcomers
(March 1969).

Below:
'Project Adam',
presented by the
International Wool
Secretariat in Paris,
was a collection of
wool clothes based
on space-age ergonomic
technology. The suit
worn by Dennis Myers
was designed to 'give
the wearer room to
move and at the same
time to get rid of the
heat his surplus energy
generates' – somewhat
at odds with the heavily
frilled shirt (1968).

Below:
Cover of *Sir*, the men's
fashion journal, showing
a sharp Continental
silhouette and panama
hat (1967).

Opposite:
Savile Row's resistance
to change and to
newcomers without
traditional tailoring
training was finally
overcome by Tommy
Nutter, an untrained
salesman in the
Burlington Arcade, who
set up bespoke premises
on Savile Row. He
employed skilled cutters
to make his three-piece
suits: long in the waist
with wide lapels. Here
he mixes and matches
Prince of Wales check
and houndstooth with
his signature braiding
around the edge
of the jacket, worn
with correspondents
(February 1973).

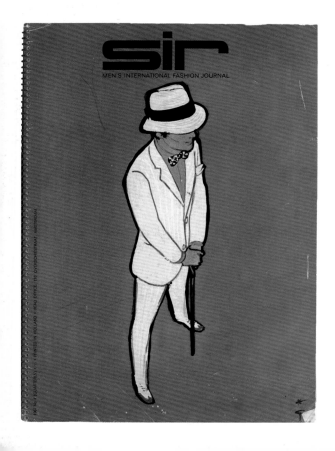

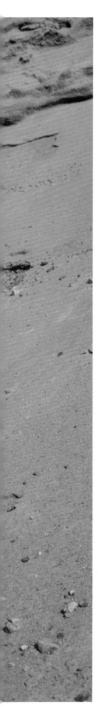

Far left:
A bleached denim safari suit by Aljack of Montreal (1971).

Left:
On opening his first Rive Gauche boutique in Paris, Yves Saint Laurent, formerly assistant to Christian Dior, declared he wanted to 'free men from their shackles, like women had just done'. His unisex gaberdine safari suits expressed his cross-gender philosophy, also epitomized by 'le smoking', a tuxedo for women that established the trouser suit as a fashion staple (1969).

212

1940–
Peacock

Below left:
Models at the
International Men's and
Boys' Wear Exhibition
(IMBEX) at Earls Court
wearing a John Craig
twinset and an Azzura
diamond-patterned
sweater. Both men wear
Oxford bags by Monte
Cristo, enormous bow
ties and platform shoes
(February 1973).

Below right:
Ex-Royal College of Art
student Ossie Clark, the
London fashion scene's
darling, specialized in
haute decadence. Here
he wears a python-skin
jacket, long hair and
Aviator shades (July
1970).

Opposite:
Artist Mark Lancaster
in an Ossie Clark shirt
with a Celia Birtwell
(Clark's wife) print and
teardrop collar (early
1970s).

1940—
MEDIA STAR

Right:
British-born Cary
Grant was much
admired by audiences
for his consummate
elegance, even when
under serious pressure,
as here in Alfred
Hitchcock's *North by
Northwest*. He had six
identical suits made
by Kilgour, French &
Stanbury for this role
(1959).

Film and fashion, like music and fashion, are intimately connected, never more so than in the decades after World War II. In our celebrity-driven culture, film stars act as conduits through which fashion can be disseminated, a fact long recognized by designers, many of whom have used movies to showcase their designs, for example, Giorgio Armani's wardrobe for Richard Gere in *American Gigolo* (1980). Equally important now is a star's appearance on the red carpet at the film awards, a more visible commercial opportunity than any catwalk show. Film stars are granted front-row seats at couture shows and feature on the covers of glossy fashion magazines and in advertising campaigns. Whether fashion follows the cinema or vice versa is difficult to say but both costume and fashion designers have to address the tricky problem of the time lapse between shooting and release. Perhaps more significantly, fashion designers frequently look to cinema for inspiration: James Dean's T-shirt, jeans and blouson jacket are a constant reference; Marlon Brando's Perfecto jacket influences both designers and advertisers; while the decadent glamour of Fellini's *La Dolce Vita* (1960) informs the look, image and feel of Italian designer duo Dolce & Gabbana's brand.

The fact that Cary Grant always wore his own clothes on screen is a testament to his faultless sense of style and effortless elegance at a time when the stylist did not exist. More recent stars appear as stylish off-screen as on: Steve McQueen always looked good whether in jeans or a suit, and Michael Caine epitomized early 1960s cool, whether as himself, or as Harry Palmer in *The Ipcress File* (1965) or as Jack Carter in *Get Carter* (1971), in which his black trench coat with turned-up collar made him look as tough but more sexy than Humphrey Bogart. James Bond, in the films from *Doctor No* (1962) to *Quantum of Solace* (2008), has perfected a classic yet contemporary style, although it has to be said that there have been periods, such as the 1970s, when Bond has been a bit too fashionable, with the consequence that the films now look dated. The same cannot be said of Sean Connery's roles as 007 – his bespoke Savile Row suits with a subtle Continental twist look as contemporary today as they did then, although some of his racier casual wardrobe does not.

The 'blaxploitation' films of the early 1970s reflected the upsurge of black culture: music and style that emerged like a phoenix from the struggle for civil rights in America. John Shaft was the first black fashion icon to appear in mainstream cinema, appealing to a white audience as much as to a black one. He heralded the strong influence of black style on fashion from the 1980s onwards. At the other end of the colour spectrum, John Travolta's seedy character in *Saturday Night Fever* (1977) relaunched the white suit, a garment invested with many different meanings from pimp to sportswear and from holiday to dandy attire, and one that will

always be associated with the fictional 1920s playboy Jay Gatsby as clothed by Ralph Lauren in the 1974 film.

Refashioning history on film is a fascinating occupation for costume and fashion designer alike. There have been many films that have re-created a look that was already 'in the air': *Bonnie and Clyde* (1967) was produced at a time when the 1920s were an important influence on fashion, *Doctor Zhivago*

(1965) made maxi-coats fashionable for both sexes in the late 1960s. Futuristic films can also influence style: for example, Ridley Scott's *Blade Runner* (1982), while reflecting 1940s glamour, seminal in the 1980s, projected it into a future dystopian vision of Los Angeles. Though Harrison Ford's clothes were not especially noticeable, the general look and feel of the *mise en scène* has a perennial attraction for architects and designers alike.

The media's power to sell fashion, indeed to create it, is undeniable: from Cary Grant's 'London Look' suits to *The Blues Brothers*' Ray-Bans (or Tom Cruise's in *Top Gun*) to Nick Kamen's Red Tab button-fly Levi's (a campaign that increased flagging sales of 501s by 700 per cent), film and TV wield great influence. In the last 20 years, a digital revolution has dissolved geographical and cultural boundaries, disseminating fashion to global audiences.

Right:
Fellini's *La Dolce Vita*
introduced not only the
word paparazzi but also
the Continental look
to a wider audience.
Marcello Mastroianni's
decadent glamour
– white suits with dark
shirts and habitual dark
glasses – is an image
constantly referenced
by fashion editors and
designers such as Dolce
& Gabbana in their
advertising campaigns
(1960).

Below:
Oscar-winning costume
designers Ann Roth
and Gary Jones
brilliantly captured
the Continental look
in Anthony Minghella's
The Talented Mr Ripley.
Jude Law as Dickie
Greenleaf exuded
elegance as the doomed
American playboy
(1999).

Right:
Cockney Michael Caine was one of a breed of new stars in Britain – the working-class hero, or as was often the case with Caine's roles, the anti-hero. Tailored by Dougie Hayward, he presents a modern image in tune with Swinging London in the 1960s and even manages to make horn-rimmed glasses look sexy (1966).

Opposite:
After his role in *The Great Escape* (1963) Steve McQueen became known as 'Mr Cool', and ever since has been consistently voted one of the world's best-dressed men. In *The Thomas Crown Affair*, one of the most stylish films of the 1960s, he proved he could wear a suit as well as dusty cowboy gear (1968).

CASINO ROYALE

Opposite:
Sean Connery's
suave elegance
underpinned his roles
as the quintessential
gentleman secret agent
James Bond. Clad in
everything from Savile
Row suits to a baby-blue
towelling all-in-one
top and shorts, Bond
represented a new
image of masculinity,
especially in the navy
shantung-silk Nehru
jacket he borrowed
from Doctor No. A style
developed by Gilbert
Féruch and Pierre
Cardin, the Nehru was
a semi-formal jacket
that did not require a
tie (1962).

Left:
Daniel Craig's suits for
Casino Royale, designed
by Lindy Hemming,
were commissioned
from leading Italian
tailor Brioni Roma.
Handmade shirts
from Turnbull &
Asser; shoes and boots
from John Lobb of St
James's; and specially
made underwear by
Sunspel of Nottingham,
completed a wardrobe
fit for 007 (2006).

1940–
Media Star

Opposite:
As small-time gangster
Clyde Barrow in *Bonnie
and Clyde*, Warren
Beatty's pinstripe suits
and cloth cap harmonized
with the nostalgia for
the 1920s (1967).

Below:
Playing two petty crooks
from Marseilles in
Borsalino, Alain Delon
and Jean-Paul Belmondo
made the most of 1930s
gangster style, strongly
associated with Italian
Borsalino hats, the
height of gangster chic
(1970).

Right:
Self-professed
godfather of soul James
Brown in a calf-length
leather coat. The civil
rights movement in
America promoted
a new awareness of
ethnic heritage and
black cool, mediated
by musicians and
actors (March 1971).

Opposite right:
Poster for the film *Shaft*.
A leather-clad Richard
Roundtree stars in the
cult movie with musical
score by Isaac Hayes.
It brought black style
to the forefront: Shaft
was 'hotter than Bond
and cooler than Bullitt'
(1971).

Opposite left:
The look was revisited
in the Matrix films
(here, in *The Matrix
Reloaded*) in which
Laurence Fishburne
appears as Morpheus
in a full-length alligator
coat (2003).

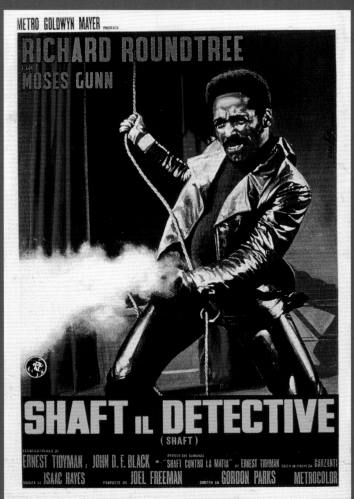

Previous spread:
John Travolta, disco dancer extraordinaire, put the sex back into suits, even the white polyester variety, in his portrayal of Tony Manero in hit movie *Saturday Night Fever* (1977).

Right:
Ralph Lauren created Robert Redford's wardrobe in the film version of F. Scott Fitzgerald's 1926 novel *The Great Gatsby*. Fitzgerald describes Jay Gatsby's obsession with clothes, sent over to him twice a year by a man in England: 'shirts with stripes and scrolls and plaids in coral and apple-green and lavender and faint orange, with monograms of Indian blue' (1974).

Opposite left:
Novelist and modern-day dandy Tom Wolfe wears his trademark white suit with a starched wing-collar formal shirt, black tie, homburg, cane and carnation. Like Mark Twain, his preference for white references his southern heritage. An acute observer of all things sartorial, he uses clothes in his 1988 novel *The Bonfire of the Vanities* to symbolize his WASP protagonist's rise and fall in the murky world of financial dealing in 1980s New York (November 1998).

Opposite right:
Sean 'P. Diddy' Combs arrives at the annual P. Diddy White Party on 4 July in New York. Accessorizing with quantities of diamond jewelry and a white trilby, he is every inch the black/white dandy gangsta (2004).

He's the
highest paid
lover in
Beverly Hills.

He leaves
women feeling
more alive
than they've
ever felt
before.

Except one.

American Gigolo

Paramount Pictures Presents A Freddie Fields Production A Film by Paul Schrader Richard Gere in "American Gigolo"
Lauren Hutton Executive Producer Freddie Fields Produced by Jerry Bruckheimer Music Composed by Giorgio Moroder
Written and Directed by Paul Schrader Original Soundtrack Recording on Polydor Records and Tapes A Paramount Picture

R RESTRICTED Read the Dell Book "Call Me" performed by Blondie   BY PARAMOUNT PICTURES CORPORATION. ALL RIGHTS RESERVED

Opposite:
Savvy detectives
Starsky and Hutch, the
first cops not to wear
suits, sported casual
streetwise clothes:
denim, leather jackets
and chunky Navaho
knits (1975–79).

Left:
Increasingly TV
and film promoted
contemporary fashion,
using fashion designers
rather than studio
costume designers
to clothe the main
characters. Indeed,
Giorgio Armani's
wardrobe for Julian
Kay, played by
Richard Gere in the
film *American Gigolo*,
defined the character,
whose fetishistic
attachment to his softly
tailored suits and fluid
shirtings recalled Jay
Gatsby. The sexually
ambiguous overtones of
the movie made Gere an
icon for male and female
viewers, and its success
put Armani squarely on
the global fashion map
(1980).

Opposite:
Clad in the latest
menswear by Armani,
Versace and Hugo
Boss, undercover
cops, Crockett and
Tubbs, lived fast
and dangerously
in *Miami Vice*. While
Tubbs (Philip Michael
Thomas) favoured
more classic tailoring,
Crockett (Don Johnson)
wore casual suits with
pastel T-shirts, shoulder
pads, rolled-up sleeves
and no socks (1984–89).

Left:
Don Johnson as
Crockett in *Miami
Vice*. The pushed-up
sleeve became not
only a possibility
through softer fabrics
and tailoring, but
also a sartorial emblem
of 1980s fashion
(1984–89).

Below left:
Perfectly groomed, Nick Kamen, the model in the Levi's ad, expressed a sexual ambiguity that reflected the 'new man', whether straight or gay: the target for magazine publishers and advertising companies who quickly latched on to commercial opportunities resulting from the shift in sexual politics. The Gay Liberation Movement resulted in the recognition of the purchasing power of the 'pink pound', while the straight 'new man' would eventually become the metrosexual, celebrating fashion and grooming products as never before (1987).

Below right:
With Marvin Gaye's classic 'I Heard it Through the Grapevine' playing in the background, Nick Kamen strips off his 501 Levi's in a 1950s-style laundromat in front of an audience. The hugely successful Levi's ad campaign appealed to men and women alike, reversing the stereotypical focus of the male gaze (1985).

Opposite:
Blues Brothers Dan Aykroyd and John Belushi, the original men in black (1980), in cool suits, narrow ties and trilbies, re-established Ray-Bans as iconic eyewear.

Developed for pilots before World War II, they became popular when worn by General MacArthur in the Philippines. Heavy and dark, Wayfarers exude an air of menace and have featured in many movies, from *The Wild One* (1953) onwards.

Following spread:
Quentin Tarantino's hoodlums in *Reservoir Dogs* set about causing mayhem dressed in sharp black suits by the French designer Agnès b. They also wear Wayfarers – Aviators, as worn by Tom Cruise in *Top Gun* (1986), also remain a popular classic (1992).

1940—
CULTURE
CLUBBER

Below:
'Boy' T-shirt by
Vivienne Westwood.
Anarchy and outrage
were keywords
for punk, the most
dynamic, subversive
and influential fashion
movement since World
War II (c. 1977).

Zoot suiters, Teddy boys, mods, rockers, skinheads and hippies were among the 'style tribes' that continued into the 1970s and have never disappeared. Designers and fashion editors re-create these looks endlessly and mix them up to create new styles, while a host of club nights and festivals enable social gatherings of the like-minded. Interwoven with these, glam rock appeared on the scene in the early 1970s in the ever-changing form of David Bowie and its greatest protagonist Marc Bolan, whose clothes seemed less *costume* than Bowie's. Mick Jagger wore eye make-up in the 1960s, but it was Bolan and his cross-dressing antics who made it possible for men to wear glitter on their cheeks and stacked snakeskin platform shoes. Yet it was another musical genre that emerged from the underground clubs of New York and London in the mid 1970s that announced one of the most influential street styles ever seen. With its deliberate 'in your face' shock tactics, punk was the result of a dynamic creative collaboration between music impresario Malcolm McLaren (who had previously managed the New York Dolls) and his then partner Vivienne Westwood. McLaren's British band The Sex Pistols outraged the public with their blend of offensive behaviour, anarchic music and provocative clothes emblazoned with seditious motifs and subversive logos, designed by Westwood and sold in her shop, World's End, in King's Road. Customized T-shirts, studded black leather, bondage trousers with attached 'nappies' and rubber fetish wear

were embellished with the notorious safety pins and other found objects in a collage designed to provoke and shock.

Punk was a short-lived style that was soon, like Carnaby Street before it, destined to become a clichéd tourist attraction. Again, it was a look appropriated by commercialism, though never a serious challenge to mainstream fashion. Westwood, informed by an increasingly intellectual approach to her work, designed her 'Pirate' collection (Autumn/Winter 1981–82), a mix of highwayman dandy and buccaneer that launched the New Romantic style of the early 1980s. Punk was the final hurrah of the power of subcultural styles to shock: during the 1980s, as in the 1960s, London once again became a magnet for designers

Left:
The mods, symbolized
by the parka and
scooter, were demonized
by the press after a
series of confrontations
with rockers on Bank
Holiday Mondays at
seaside resorts in the
South and East of
England (1964).

searching for inspiration. As a result, fashion, like musical genres, fragmented into a myriad of styles, each with its own dedicated band of followers.

Diametrically opposed to the self-conscious posturing of the New Romantics, goths, latter-day punks and indeed the pumped-up power-dressing 1980s city slicker, break dancers and rappers brought a new musical genre – hip hop – to the

fore. They adopted sportswear: hoodies, designer tracksuits, baseball jackets, long shorts, T-shirts, baseball caps (worn backwards) and lavish gold and diamond jewelry. Acid house ravers, New Age travellers, eco-warriors and grunge followers all developed signature looks at that time too, but it is black style and music that has since dominated our sartorial and musical culture.

244

Culture Clubber

Right above:
Paul Weller, arbiter
of 1980s mod style,
in a herringbone
tweed overcoat causes
consternation among
his fans who are
dressed in a more
stereotypical mod
style (1984).

Right below:
As is often the
case, nostalgic
reinterpretations of
a fashion can seem
to be more authentic
than the original.
Here, new mods wear
sharp-cut Continental
shiny mohair suits
with narrow 1960s
ties, loafers and white
socks (1980).

Opposite:
A member of the New
Untouchables, a global
organization that
promotes mod and 1960s
culture. Congregating
at seaside locations on
Bank Holiday Mondays,
they translate the look
of their forebears
through music, dress
and accessories into
a modern idiom (2002).

Following spread:
Skinheads evolved
from the 1960s 'hard'
mods. Their natural
enemies were the
hippies whom they
regarded as flash
effete middle-class
intellectuals. Some
expressed their hostility
to society on the football
terraces and through
fascist and racist
politics, cementing
their reputation as
troublemakers (1969).

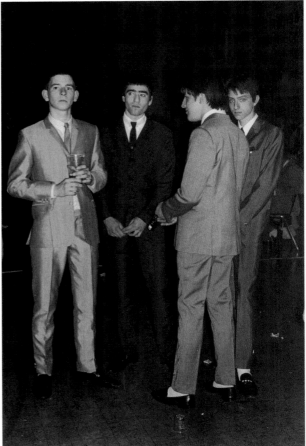

Opposite:
The skinhead 'uniform' consisted of denim or off-white Levi Sta-Prest jeans supported by clip-on braces, a button-down Ben Sherman shirt, sheepskin coat or Harrington jacket, a pork pie hat and heavy brogues worn with white or red socks or 'bovver' boots (Dr Martens or cherry reds). Smarter skinhead wear included 'tonic' suits (made of two-tone mohair) and a Crombie fly-front overcoat with velvet collar (1970).

Left above:
The Sharpies were a suburban East Melbourne gang whose 'well-dressed thuggery' combined elements of mod, skinhead and hippie style – known as 'bogun'. They wore handmade shoes, tight Levi's, cardigans and caps, had mullet haircuts and listened to AC/DC and Suzi Quatro (1973).

Left below:
The involvement of some skinheads with nationalist politics is perhaps the reason why, unlike other subcultural styles, it is rarely revisited by fashion designers, though die-hards continue to wear the uniform (1980s).

Right:
As Ziggy Stardust,
one of his many stage
personae, glam-rock
star David Bowie
crossed gender
boundaries with
meticulously crafted
stage wear, make-up
and hairstyles. Here he
wears his 'Woodland
Creatures' costume
designed by Kansai
Yamamoto (1973).

Opposite:
David Bowie in a
handmade yellow suit
by Freddie Buretti, who
also designed costumes
for Ziggy Stardust
(c. 1974).

1940–
Culture Clubber

Right:
'Cock rocker' Marc
Bolan of T.Rex at
home in skintight velvet
trousers, chequered
platform shoes and a
ballet cardigan. Bolan
read Beau Brummell's
biography as a child and
was a self-confessed
dandy, visiting every
subcultural style from
mod onwards. He
became the proto-glam
rocker; his androgynous
looks, heightened
by glitter, eyeshadow
and feather boas,
inspired a generation
of performers and fans
to glam up (c. 1975).

Opposite:
Indicative of the 1970s
taste for nostalgia,
Bryan Ferry's suit was
tailored by London
designer Antony Price,
a longstanding Roxy
Music collaborator.
Price's signature
padded shoulders
and sharp cut owe an
aesthetic debt to the
1940s, albeit the era
romanticized and
dandified through
gangster films and pulp-
fiction imagery (1976).

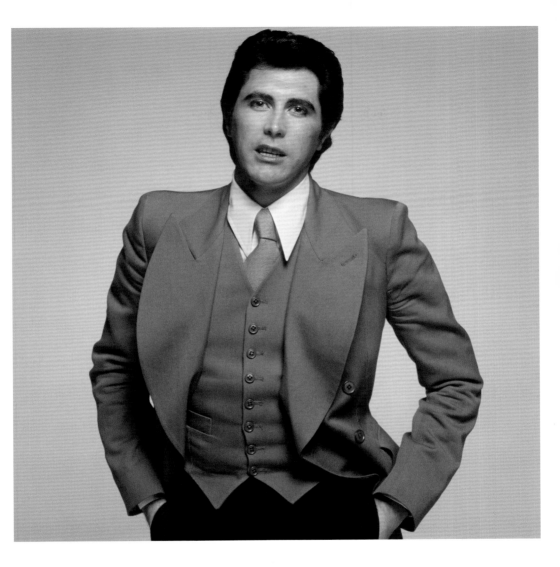

254

1940–
Culture Clubber

Right:
Malcolm McLaren, manager of The Sex Pistols and co-owner with partner Vivienne Westwood of SEX, a shop in the King's Road that started life as the cult fashion destination Hung On You in the 1960s. The shop went through many incarnations and names, first selling 1950s Teddy boy gear, then 1960s rocker leather, then fetish wear. Westwood's exploration of innovative cutting and daring materials made the shop the powerhouse of the punk movement (December 1976).

Opposite:
One of the most important garments of the punk movement, Westwood's Anarchy shirt was appliquéd with a label depicting Karl Marx and printed with black hands and the Italian fascist slogan 'We are not afraid of ruins' (1977).

Opposite:
The juxtaposition
of patriotic and
Nazi symbols, an
ironic commentary
on the hypocrisy
of establishment
values and part of the
iconography of punk,
was more subversive
than that of the 1960s
when the Union
Jack, red buses and
uniformed bobbies
symbolized Swinging
London (1977).

Left:
Johnny Rotten of
The Sex Pistols in
Westwood shirt and
bondage trousers.
After punk, the power
to shock through dress
dissipated; never again
would clothing be so
disturbing (1977).

1940–
Culture Clubber

Below:
A modern-day
Japanese punk with
all the stereotypical
accoutrements,
including a dip-dyed
Mohican haircut,
symbol of the style
worldwide.

Right:
Punks in Tallinn,
Estonia. As punk
was commercialized,
Westwood and
McLaren moved on,
but it remains a style
endlessly referenced
by designers and
contemporary youth
subcultures (c. 1989).

Right:
Club impresario
Chris Sullivan
wearing flamboyant
buccaneer style: a
pirate shirt, zouave
trousers, a studded
belt, bandanas, and a
cat-o'-nine-tails whip.
The New Romantics
met up at a series
of weekly club nights
in and around Soho
where art students,
music aficionados and
designers mingled. It
was a self-conscious
style, predicated
on dressing up and
striking a pose (1980).

Opposite:
Milliner Stephen Jones,
whose creations for
Dior now grace John
Galliano's catwalks
(one can be seen on the
block beside him), in
a restrained grey suit,
white shirt with the
collar turned up and
Beau Brummell-style
cravat (1980).

Opposite:
A New Romantic in full piratical gear (1981).

Left:
Goths gathered in the Batcave, a Saturday club night at Gossips in London's Soho. Darker and more sinister than the New Romantics, the goths combined aspects of punk with occult overtones (1981).

Right:
Post punk, Vivienne Westwood's seminal 'Pirate' collection introduced a more romantic historicism. Never shy of crossing gender boundaries in her work, Westwood designed this outfit to be unisex (1980–81).

Far right:
Napoleonic pantomime buccaneer, pirate and highwayman, Adam Ant took the look into the popular mainstream, here in the garb he wore for pop video *Goody Two Shoes* (1983).

Below:
Culture Club singer Boy George and boyfriend Marilyn drag themselves up for a night out clubbing in London (1982).

Opposite:
During the 1980s, London's gay scene flourished: here Boy George faces the press in confrontational style (1986).

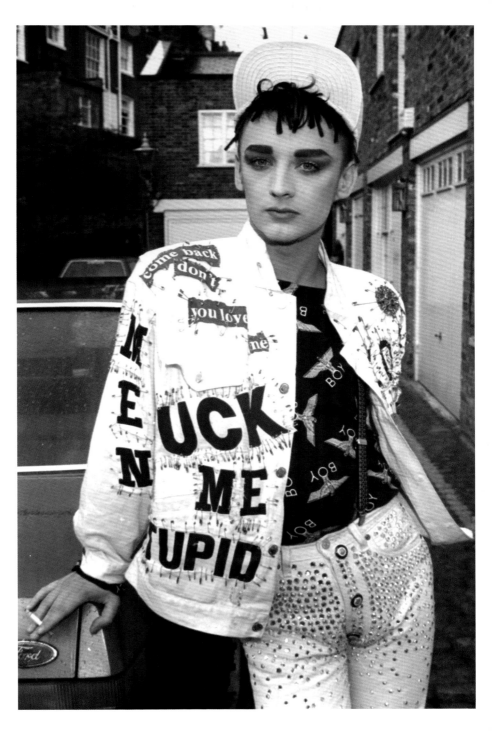

Opposite:
Break dancers on
the street in the
uniform of hip hop
and rap. Branded
trainers, baseball caps,
tracksuits and hoodies
all derived from early
sportswear, though
by now it was the labels
and logos rather than
the team colours that
were all-important
(c. 1983).

Below:
Run-DMC, chart-
busting hip-hop band
in logo leather, trilbies,
shades and chunky gold
chains. In 1986 they
released a single called
'My Adidas' (1987).

Left:
Basketball star Tracy McGrady in an Adidas tracksuit (2002).

Below:
Hip-hop and R & B superstar Pharrell (left) and his collaborator, Japanese designer Nigo, at the MTV Music Awards in New York. Clothing lines are now as profitable as music: P. Diddy's Sean John label, Jay-Z's Rocawear, Kanye West's Pastelle line and Pharrell's duo Billionaire Boys Club and Ice Cream attest to the intimate relationship between music and fashion. BBC is a spin on classic Ralph Lauren, while Ice Cream is couture skate; Pharrell's clothes are expensive, a fact perhaps ironically alluded to by the dollar-sign bling (2006).

Right:
Typical acid-house garb: a fluorescent psychedelic shirt and a smiley T-shirt. The smiley became the symbol of the raver's ecstasy-fuelled underground dance culture during the second Summer of Love (1988).

Opposite above left:
Clandestine raves, music festivals, the summer solstice, squats, tents and caravans were the haunts of eco-warriors and New Age travellers. Dressed in patchwork layers of torn jeans, rainbow woolly jumpers, fleeces and gypsy hats, they embraced the dream of Aquarius with a new commitment to ecological and environmental issues (1990s).

Opposite above right:
Pixie, a member of the Expanding Invisible Collective travelling community, wears a fleece, an ethnic bead choker and a felted wool hat with moss trim (2001).

Opposite below:
Cover of *The Face* magazine. Kurt Cobain of cult indie band Nirvana epitomized grunge – long hair, stripey shirts and jeans. Grunge expressed through music and anti-fashion the anxiety felt during the early 1990s, a time of economic depression, political instability and war in the Middle East (1993).

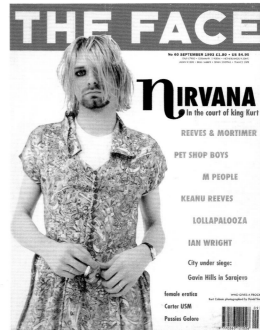

THE FACE

No 60 SEPTEMBER 1993 £1.80 · US $4.95
ITALY L7900 · GERMANY 11.90DM · NETHERLANDS 9.50HFL
JAPAN ¥1390 · BELG 166BFR · SPAIN 500PTAS · FRANCE 28FR

nIRVANA
In the court of king Kurt

REEVES & MORTIMER

PET SHOP BOYS

M PEOPLE

KEANU REEVES

LOLLAPALOOZA

IAN WRIGHT

City under siege:

Gavin Hills in Sarajevo

female erotica

Carter USM

Pussies Galore

WHO GIVES A PROCK?
Kurt Cobain photographed by David Sims

09>

Opposite:
Johnny Vercoutre (right)
and David Piper are
leading lights of Time
for Tea and The Modern
Times Club, nostalgic
re-creations of all things
vintage and burlesque
from the 1920s to the
1950s (2004).

Left:
Amechi Ihenacho,
London fashion editor
of *Flux* magazine,
a Manchester-based
independent arts
publication launched
in 1997, at Time for
Tea (2004).

1940—
STYLIST

Below:
Ray Petri, driving force behind the style cooperative Buffalo. Petri's styling of men in skirts inspired Jean Paul Gaultier to make them a constant feature of his work (1987).

Opposite:
Cover of *The Face* magazine, with photography by Jamie Morgan. Felix, in herringbone tweed jacket, polo-neck sweater with a feather and a 'killer' label stuck in its band, was styled by Petri for a spread titled 'The Harder they Come'. Traditional images of masculinity and conventional approaches to fashion photography were subverted by Buffalo's androgynous models and experimental styling (March 1985).

IN the 1980s the concept of the 'new man' emerged, largely as a response to Gay Liberation and a rash of style magazines, some explicitly homoerotic in their approach to male fashion. *The Face*, *Blitz*, *I-D* and *Arena* were all launched in the early to mid 1980s: manuals of streetstyle that were the antithesis of the glossies in their creative approach to dressing. Stylists such as Ray Petri, Simon Foxton and Judy Blame worked with a coterie of photographers, journalists and models to create influential spreads that encapsulated the trend towards a new self-fashioning of the male image, often by confounding stereotypical expectations of gay subcultural dress. Petri's work in particular was seminal – his vision was eclectic, constituting a bricolage of tailoring, designer wear, ethnic, sporting, historical, subcultural and streetstyle elements that redefined men's fashion. He made the World War II American Air Force MA-1 nylon flight jacket (with orange lining originally intended to be used as a distress signal) the 'uniform' of Buffalo. Teamed with Levi's 501s and Dr Martens, the ensemble became the signature style of gay clones and, confusingly, also of 1980s skinheads. His Buffalo cooperative not only spawned a generation of fashion creatives, image makers and writers whose influence is still felt in contemporary culture but also established the position of the stylist as an essential contributor to the fashion process.

THE FACE **No. 59**

● MARCH 1985 85p US $2.75

GERMANY 5.80 DM

THE FACE

KILLER

SAM SHEPARD AND JESSICA LANGE
HOLLYWOOD'S HOT COUPLE

**Alison Moyet
Andy Warhol
Lovers rock
Pogues ◆ Brazil
Mel Smith**

H A R D

Photo Jamie Morgan

278

Below:
Arena magazine's
'Ragamuffin'
photographic sequence
(unpublished) by Martin
Brading. The model
on the left wears a flight
jacket, football shirt,
panama and Peruvian
hat: non-fashion with
attitude, aptly titled
'Tough me Tough'.
Simon de Montford
(right) wears a mix
of flea-market and
designer clothes. Given
the title 'Yard Style
– Easy Skanking', the
photo is a reference to
Jamaican culture, one
of the many influences
Petri absorbed (1987).

Opposite:
Another photo from the
'Ragamuffin' sequence.
The model wears
Peruvian knitwear,
a sheepskin cap and
a suede blouson jacket
(1987).

Right:
Early issues of *The Face*,
which was essentially
a music publication,
did not include fashion
spreads, but featured
people with style,
such as identical
twins Chuka and
Dubem Okonkwo, here
dressed as 1960s Rude
Boys, Jamaica's first
subcultural streetstyle.
The look migrated
via ska and reggae to
London, where the Hard
Mods, skinheads and
Two Tone movements
in turn adapted it (1980).

1940–
Stylist

Right:
I-D 'Strictly'. This
shoot by Jason Evans,
styled by Simon Foxton,
features the 'straight-up'
style of photography.
In a parody of English
country gentlemen,
Foxton dresses his
models in traditional
sporting garb and
sets them against a
suburban backdrop,
exploring issues of
cultural, ethnic and
political identity.
Here, the model wears
a riding jacket and
plus twos by Swaine
& Adeney (Savile Row
suppliers of hunting kit),
shoes from Trickers and
a monocle from Chanel
(1991).

Left:
From the same photo
shoot, a model wears a
hunting pink jacket by
Ghanaian-born designer
Joe Casely-Hayford,
who trained in Savile
Row, teamed with
corduroy jeans by Rich
and Strange and riding
boots. This is a modern
interpretation of Beau
Brummell's style, and
the shoot is headed up
by one of the dandy's
dictums: 'No perfumes
... but very fine linen,
plenty of it and country
washing. If John Bull
turns round to look after
you, you are not well
dressed, but either too
stiff, too tight or too
fashionable' (1991).

1940—
DESIGNER

The 1980s witnessed the emergence of designers such as Ralph Lauren, Calvin Klein and Giorgio Armani, who began to feature menswear on an equal basis to womanswear in their collections, recognizing its increasing potential as a force in the consumption of fashion. Lauren heads an empire with a dozen brand names built on a nostalgic evocation of British tailoring, retro sportswear (he is the official outfitter for Wimbledon), American Ivy League and cowboys of the Great West. His stores are decorated as a complete lifestyle package: leather chesterfields, antique sporting prints, roaring fires and Navaho blankets give the impression of a gentleman's club or a lodge on the prairie. His fellow New Yorker and near contemporary Calvin Klein built his globally successful brand on the back of jeans, underpants and perfumes. Initially a minimalist womenswear designer, he launched into menswear and jeans in 1977 and into men's underwear in 1982. Throughout the 1980s and 1990s, Klein's and Lauren's seminal advertising campaigns, shot by the likes of Richard Avedon and Bruce Weber, often using celebrities as models, ensured worldwide publicity.

Giorgio Armani began his career in fashion at the Italian department store La Rinascente and went on to found his own menswear label in 1975. He revolutionized tailoring in the 1980s, removing the stiff interlining of suits and making them with fluid fabrics such as linens and ultra-light wools, some previously only used for women's garments. The favourite tailor of celebrities, he, unusually, retains sole control of his vast empire, which has expanded into the lifestyle market, including home furnishings and chocolates.

Many designers have been inspired and influenced by streetstyle rather than carefully

evolving a 'line'. Jean Paul Gaultier, often referred to as the 'enfant terrible' of French couture, designed his first menswear collection in 1984, since when he has consistently explored gender boundaries in his work, dressing men in skirts, and featuring androgynous models in advertising campaigns. He was a frequent visitor to London in the 1980s, where he plundered the vibrant club culture, street markets and style shops for inspiration.

Also in the 1980s, an influx of Japanese designers to Paris introduced new concepts of dressing. Yohji Yamamoto and Rei Kawakubo of Comme des Garçons designed clothes that redefined the body shape: outsized, asymmetrical, loose, layered, baggy and nearly always black. Their intellectual approach and deconstructivist detailing – unfinished edges, holes, tatters and external details such as the loop on the back of Yamamoto's jackets – inspired the work of the Antwerp Six, the group of Belgian designers that includes Martin Margiela and Dries Van Noten, who also challenge conventional practices of garment making and traditional ideas of masculinity.

British designers continue to contribute their unique vision: Vivienne Westwood pushes the boundaries of menswear through intellectual rigour and absolute belief in the power of clothes to express individuality. She looks to the past for her inspiration; her themed collections often feature daringly innovative tailoring using traditional British fabrics in her own inimitable style. Her menswear line, MAN, launched in 1996 and shown in Milan, is designed in collaboration with her husband Andreas Kronthaler. From lowly beginnings in the early 1970s in a backstreet shop in Nottingham, Sir Paul Smith now runs a global empire that is Britain's highest-grossing designer business. Giving classic clothes a twist and combining them with an eclectic mix of accessories, displayed in a curiosity-shop/ art-gallery setting, Smith expresses a playful attitude that is nevertheless underlined by quality and craftsmanship.

The suit survives, indeed thrives, in the hands of designers such as Raf Simons, Hedi Slimane, Jil Sander and Tom Ford. Skinny trousers, tightly cut jackets and narrow ties all recall the slim, sharp *bella figura* silhouette of minimalism in the 1960s. Others, such as New Yorker Thom Browne, continue to explore, manipulate and alter the basic format of the suit by looking at styles of the past, for example, Browne's pea coat, a popular jacket style during the nineteenth century.

While tailors have maintained their traditional position as purveyors of bespoke luxury, fashion designers are now also regarded as haute couturiers of the male wardrobe, with prices that match bespoke tailoring, even for ready-to-wear suits. The suit may well survive for another 350 years: it has never been surpassed as the all-purpose, universally accepted garment and essence of masculine style. Fashion is temporary but style, like the suit, is enduring.

Left:
Jean Paul Gaultier's
modern take on an
eighteenth-century
woman's quilted
petticoat demonstrates
his blurring of traditional
gender boundaries
(photograph by Paolo
Roversi, 1985).

288

1940–
Designer

Right:
Ralph Lauren Purple
Label suit for Autumn/
Winter 2002–03; sharp
tailoring with 1930s
curves and detailing
(2002).

Opposite above:
Ralph Lauren outside
his London flagship
store on Bond Street
kitted out in cowboy
style: top-to-toe denim
and a Navaho turquoise
and silver belt (1981).

Opposite below:
Ralph Lauren's
advertising campaigns
broke new ground.
Photographed in black
and white as narrative
sequences, many shot
by Bruce Weber, they
became iconic images
of the age, while looking
back at the past (1990s).

POLO RALPH LAUREN

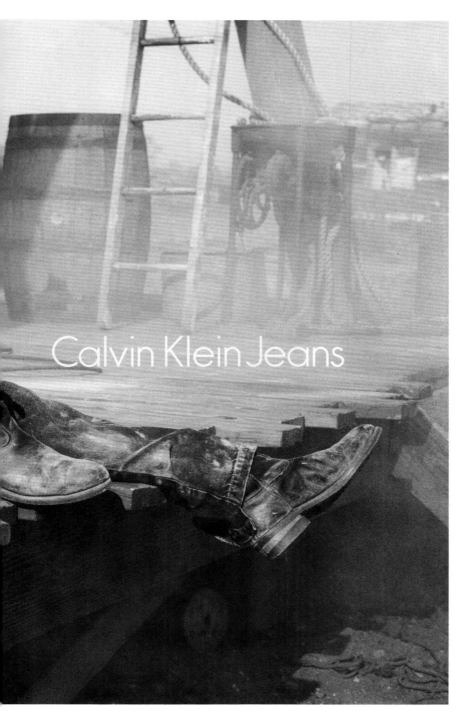

Left:
Advertisement for
Calvin Klein jeans,
represented as sweat-
stained workwear,
but the ultimate in
expensive designer
chic (2005).

Opposite:
A bronzed Calvin Klein epitomized his own target customer, the 1980s 'new man'. His perfume, cK, launched in 1993, was the first unisex fragrance (1983).

Left above:
Rapper LL Cool J wearing his Calvin Kleins (the name is now synonymous with the garment) as they should be worn – with the waistband showing (1999).

Left below:
Advertisement for Calvin Klein's Contradiction fragrance for men (1999).

Contradiction
for men
introducing a new fragrance from
Calvin Klein

Opposite:
Armani suits for
Spring/Summer 2006.
Soft, slippery fabrics in
a muted colour palette
continue Armani's
exploration of tailoring
(2005).

Below left:
Giorgio Armani, the
master of understated
tailoring (2007).

Below right:
Armani's soft suits:
while 'hanger appeal'
is lacking, they are
celebrated for their
uniquely comfortable
cut and minimalism
(1987).

Below left:
A silver wrapped short skirt with Egyptian-style pleats by Jean Paul Gaultier for Spring/Summer 2008 (2007).

Below right:
Jean Paul Gaultier snapped in Camden Market, then a favourite hunting ground for fashion aficionados. He wears his trademark matelot sweater and a platinum quiff (1987).

Opposite:
Jean Paul Gaultier brought streetstyle to the catwalk, applying a mix of high camp and wit to his eclectic collections, which include gangster-style suits, fetish wear, sarongs, skirts and the Highland kilt. Sailor chic remains one of his most iconic looks, revisited here at his thirtieth-anniversary retrospective (2006).

298

1940–
Designer

Opposite:
Yohji Yamamoto's menswear, here from his Autumn/Winter 1986–87 collection, encapsulates concepts of use, familiarity and the patina of age. Inspired by German photographer August Sander's early twentieth-century images of working men, he believes in real clothes, rather than fashion.

Right above:
Masatomo continues the tradition of minimalist Japanese design: an oversized floor-length black coat that disguises rather than conceals the body is accessorized with a wide-brimmed panama and a suitcase (2002).

Right below:
Yohji Yamamoto all in black (2008).

Following spread left:
Dries Van Noten's Autumn/Winter 1987–88 collection 'Rich Man Poor Man' drew on English fashion from around 1890. Shown here is his bravura combination of stripes and checks in the season's colour palette of rich dark browns and Bordeaux (1987).

Following spread right:
Entirely made in traditional British fabrics such as Harris Tweed and Liberty prints, Van Noten's collection contrasted perfect tailoring with unexpected combinations of colour and pattern – his trademark. Here, a Harris Tweed jacket and Fair Isle waistcoat are paired with voluminous striped trousers (1987).

Below left:
Gurkha/Highland
warrior meets urban
punk in Galliano's
Spring/Summer 2009
collection for men
(2008).

Below right:
Galliano revels in
the performance of
fashion. After each
show he appears
dressed as a character
in his own masquerade;
here in boho/hobo
chic patchwork coat,
matching fedora and
spotted train (2005).

Opposite:
Martin Margiela
is known for his
theoretical approach
to fashion: his
'deconstructivist'
techniques and
assembly of decayed
or vintage materials
challenge accepted
notions of fashion.
This jacket for his
Autumn/Winter
2006–07 collection
is made of ski gloves:
recycling as high
fashion (2006).

Right:
Vivienne Westwood's Autumn/Winter 2008–09 collection featured a glen plaid suit with retro styling on the top half, but with an unmistakably modern twist to the loose crotch trousers, which recall her reign as the queen of punk (2008).

Below:
Vivienne Westwood surrounded by models at her Milan Autumn/Winter 2008–09 show (2008).

Opposite left:
Alexander McQueen's Autumn/Winter 2008–09 collection includes a range of layered separates through which he explores new cutting techniques: here a plaid jacket is wrapped around the body and tightly buttoned over a longer fringed waistcoat (2008).

Opposite right:
A checked jacket is overlaid by an additional half jacket slipping off the shoulder, attached at each hip and held in place by a large safety pin on one side. Although McQueen has often explored themes of alienation and decay, this collection, with its rich mix of Indian embroidery, Kashmir shawls, Mongolian fur hats and Aztec blankets, joyfully combines tailoring and ethnic influences (2008).

Below:
Sir Paul Smith has
built his reputation
by exporting British
style (2003).

Opposite:
Paul Smith's Autumn/
Winter 2001–02
collection included
formal dinner suits
teamed with giant
checked coats, one
revealing a glimpse
of his signature
spotted lining (2001).

Below left:
German-born Jil Sander launched her first menswear line in 1997, and in 2005 Raf Simons was appointed as creative director. His purity of line fits perfectly with the ethos and image of the luxury brand (2008).

Below right:
Raf Simons combines youth style with traditional tailoring techniques. His clean modernist silhouette is expressed in this two-tone overcoat shown as part of his menswear line Raf by Raf Simons (2007).

Opposite:
Having designed for YSL Rive Gauche, Hedi Slimane was appointed creative director of Dior Homme between 2000 and 2007. Looking back at the 1960s, and inspired by contemporary music, he introduced the razor-sharp skinny silhouette that now defines much of men's fashion. His use of ultra-skinny boys caused similar criticism to that levelled at the prevalence of anorexic female models (2005).

Below left:
In 2000 the Gucci Group acquired the Yves Saint Laurent and YSL labels. Tom Ford's Autumn/Winter 2004–05 collection of ready-to-wear for Yves Saint Laurent featured classic tailoring with bright accessories (2004).

Below right:
Yves Saint Laurent ready-to-wear Autumn/Winter 2004–05 by Tom Ford (2004).

Opposite:
Tom Ford's portrait at the launch of his book *Ten Years* in New York. Between 1990 and 2004 he transformed Gucci into a multi-billion-dollar empire, making it one of the most profitable luxury brands in the world. Since 2005 his eponymous label has become known for beauty products and luxury menswear (2004).

Below:

The Septemberists Triptych. These outfits display all the design hallmarks of Thom Browne's distinctive take on menswear. Founded in the craft of hand tailoring, Browne's work twists tradition, incorporating historical elements and theatrical flourishes more readily associated with womenswear, such as bustles or trains. Although more subdued, the clothing in this triptych, taken from a film by artist Anthony Goicolea to showcase the Spring/Summer 2007 collection, shows the 'shrunken' tailoring and abbreviated proportions Browne is known for, along with his trademark cropped 'flood length' trousers (2006).

Opposite:

New York designer Thom Browne in trademark tightly cut jacket (c. 2005).

FURTHER READING

Amies, Hardy, *The Englishman's Suit*, Quartet, London, 1994

Bennett-England, Rodney, *Dress Optional: The Revolution in Menswear*, Peter Owen, London, 1967

Breward, Christopher, *The Hidden Consumer: Masculinities, Fashion and City Life 1860–1914*, Manchester University Press, Manchester, 1999

Breward, Christopher (ed.), *Fashion Theory: The Journal of Dress, Body and Culture*, 'Masculinities Special Issue', vol.4, no.4, Berg Publishers, Oxford, 2000

Byrde, Penelope, *The Male Image: Men's Fashion in England 1300–1970*, Batsford, London, 1979

Chenoune, Farid, *A History of Men's Fashion*, Flammarion, Paris, 1993

Cicolini, Alice, *The New English Dandy*, Thames & Hudson, London, 2005

Cohn, Nik, *Today There Are No Gentlemen: The Changes in Englishmen's Clothes since the War*, Weidenfeld & Nicolson, London, 1971

Davies, Hywel, *Modern Menswear*, Laurence King Publishing Limited, 2008

De Marly, Diana, *Fashion for Men: An Illustrated History*, Batsford, London, 1985

Elms, Robert, *The Way We Wore: A Life in Threads*, Picador, London, 2005

Gavenas, Mary Lisa, *The Fairchild Encyclopedia of Menswear*, Fairchild, New York, 2008

Green, Jonathan, *All Dressed Up: The Sixties and the Counterculture*, Pimlico, London, 1999

Hochswender, Woody, *Men in Style: The Golden Age of Fashion from Esquire*, Rizzoli, New York, 1993

McDowell, Colin, *The Man of Fashion: Peacock Males and Perfect Gentlemen*, Thames & Hudson, London, 1997

Martin, Richard, and Koda, Harold, *Jocks & Nerds: Men's Style in the Twentieth Century*, Rizzoli, New York, 1989

Mort, Frank, *Cultures of Consumption: Masculinities and Social Space in Late Twentieth-Century Britain*, Routledge, London, 1996

O'Neill, Alistair, *London: After A Fashion*, Reaktion, London, 2007

Osgerby, Bill, *Playboys in Paradise: Masculinity, Youth and Leisure-style in Modern America*, Berg, Oxford, 2001

Polhemus, Ted, *Streetstyle: From Sidewalk to Catwalk*, Thames & Hudson, London, 1994

Savage, Jon, *Teenage: The Creation of Youth 1875–1945*, Chatto & Windus, London, 2007

Tulloch, Carol (ed.), *Black Style*, V&A Publications, London, 2004

Walker, Richard, *The Savile Row Story*, Prion, London, 1988

INDEX

INDEX

CREDITS

Courtesy of the Advertising Archives: pp.15, 24t, 24bl, 27t, 40r, 48, 52, 56, 59t, 89, 92tr, 94t, 128, 129t, 135, 152b, 155t, 155b, 169b, 176, 195, 208, 236r, 289b, 290–1, 293b. **Courtesy Albert Khan Archive:** p.50. **The Art Archive/ Bibliothèque des Arts Décoratifs Paris/ Gianni Dagli Orti:** p.125. **The Art Archive/ Culver Pictures:** p.30. **The Art Archive/Royal Automobile Club London/NB Design:** pp.106, 107. **Austin Reed:** p.19, 24br. **Property of Biagiotti Cigna Collection:** p.73. **Martin Brading:** pp.274, 278, 279. **Camera Press:** p.185. **Courtesy of Carolyn Cassady and Penguin Books:** p.175. **Christie's Images Ltd:** p.242. **Courtesy of Condé Nast:** p.183. **Corbis © ADAGP, Paris and DACS, London 2009:** pp.132, 136l. **© Bettmann/Corbis:** pp.59b, 84l, 92l, 147t, 169t, 171, 210, 211. **© Stephane Cardinale/People Avenue/Corbis:** pp.190r, 297. **© William Coupon/Corbis:** p.292. **© Daniel Dal Zennaro/epa/Corbis:** p.295l. **© Giulio Di Mauro/epa/Corbis:** p.308l. **© Michael Freeman/Corbis:** p.162t. **© Lynn Goldsmith/ Corbis:** pp.231l, 240, 257. **© E.O. Hoppé/Corbis:** p.134. **© Hulton-Deutsch Collection/Corbis:** p.124. **© Kelly-Mooney Photography/Corbis:** p.162b. **© Andy Kingsbury/Corbis:** pp.20–1. **© Christian Kober/Robert Harding World Imagery/Corbis:** p.258. **© Daniele La Monaca/ Reuters/Corbis:** p.294. **© Kurt Markus/ Corbis:** p.168. **© Corinne Mariaud/Corbis:** p.306. **© Reuters/Corbis:** pp.288, 298t, 307. **© Stapleton Collection/Corbis:** p.105. **© Sunset Boulevard/Corbis:** p.225. **© Benoit Tessier/ Reuters/Corbis:** p.298b. **© Peter Turnley/ Corbis:** p.259. **Courtesy of David Drebin:** pp.268–9. **Courtesy Archivio Depero Rovereto:** p.75. **Courtesy of Dries Van Noten:** pp.284, 300–1. **Courtesy of Jason Evans:** pp.282, 283. **AFP/Getty Images:** pp.60–1, 62, 120. **Evan Agostini/Getty Images:** p.269. **William H. Alden/Getty Images:** p.243. **Maurice Ambler/ Getty Images:** p.172. **American Stock/Getty Images:** p.148b. **Gordon Anthony/Getty Images:** p.139. **H. Armstrong Roberts/ Retrofile/Getty Images:** p.154. **Brad Barket/ Getty Images:** p.231r. **Al Bello/Getty Images:** p.129b. **Bruce Bennett Studios/Getty Images:** p.111. **George C. Beresford/Beresford/Getty Images:** pp.26l, 102. **Bowers/Getty Images:** p.311. **Giuseppe Cacace/AFP/Getty Images:** pp.305l, 305r. **Central Press/Getty Images:** pp.96, 123, 157. **Central Press/Hulton Archive/ Getty Images:** p.209. **C.P. Curran/Hulton Archive/Getty Images:** p.51l. **Loomis Dean/ Time Life Pictures/Getty Images:** p.205l. **Debi Doss/Hulton Archive/Getty Images:** p.250. **W. & D. Downey/Getty Images:** p.13, 29, 114–15. **Frank Edwards/Fotos International/Getty Images:** p.163. **Evening Standard/Getty Images:** pp.63bl, 212r, 226. **Express/Getty Images:** pp.95, 177, 254. **Fox Photos/Getty Images:** pp.118tr, 127, 130–1. **FPG/Getty Images:** p.113. **FPG/Hulton Archive/Getty Images:** p.16. **General Photographic Agency/ Getty Images:** p.117r. **Herbert Gehr/Time Life Pictures/Getty Images:** pp.63tl, 63tr. **Allan Grant/Time Life Pictures/Getty Images:** pp.150r, 174. **Jim Gray/Keystone/Getty Images:** p.202. **François Guillot/AFP/Getty Images:** pp.302l, 302r, 309, 310l, 310r. **Peter Hall/Keystone Features/Getty Images:** p.161. **Marie Hansen/ Time Life Pictures/Getty Images:** p.147b. **Hirz/ Getty Images:** pp.10, 38r, 39. **Dave Hogan/Getty Images:** pp.264b, 265. **Dave Hogan/Hulton Archive/Getty Images:** p.236l. **Martha Holmes/Time Life Pictures/Getty Images:** p.152t. **Hulton Archive/Getty Images:** pp.23, 26r, 46–7, 54, 84r, 85, 86, 93, 94b, 98, 100t, 110, 159, 233, 267. **Anwar Hussein/Hulton Archive/ Getty Images:** p.252. **George Karger/Pix Inc./ Time Life Pictures/Getty Images:** p.151. **Roy Jones/Hulton Archive/Getty Images:** p.207. **Keystone/Getty Images:** pp.38l, 194, 248. **Keystone/Hulton Archive/Getty Images:** p.182. **John Kobal Foundation/Getty Images:** p.53. **John Kobal Foundation/Hulton Archive/ Getty Images:** pp.142, 158. **Lambert/Getty Images:** p.181. **Bob Landry/Time Life Pictures/Getty Images:** p.91. **Nina Leen/Time Life Pictures/Getty Images:** pp.63br, 153. **John McGrail/Time Life Pictures/Getty Images:** p.166. **Mansell/Time & Life Pictures/Getty Images:** pp.12, 68b, 69. **MGM Studios/Courtesy of Getty Images:** p.227r. **Douglas Miller/Getty Images:** p.148t. **Chris Moore/Catwalking/ Getty Images:** p.304r. **Moore/Fox Photos/Getty Images:** p.188b. **Chris Moorhouse/Getty Images:** p.256. **Leon Morris/Getty Images:** pp.244b, 266. **Museum of the City of New York/ Getty Images:** p.82, 90l. **Michael Ochs Archives/Getty Images:** pp.164, 165, 186. **Terry O'Neill/Hulton Archive/Getty Images:** pp.198r, 251, 253. **Paramount Pictures/ Courtesy of Getty Images:** p.167, 228–9. **W.G. Phillips/Phillips/Getty Images:** p.17. **Pictorial Parade/Getty Images:** p.112. **Picture Post/Hulton Archive/Getty Images:** p.173. **Hart Preston/Time Life Pictures/Getty Images:** p.87. **Karl Prouse/Catwalking/Getty Images:** p.308r. **Steve Pyke/Getty Images:** p.244t. **Bill Ray/Life Magazine/Time & Life Pictures/Getty Images:** p.204. **Rischgitz/Getty Images:** p.22. **Ekkehard Ritter/Imagno/Getty Images:** p.70. **Jack Robinson/Getty Images:** p.220. **Sasha/Getty Images:** p.138. **Sean Sexton/Hulton Archive/Getty Images:** p.101. **Silver Screen Collection/Hulton Archive/ Getty Images:** p.160. **Clarence Sinclair Bull/ John Kobal Foundation/Getty Images:** p.104b. **Terrence Spencer/Time Life Pictures/Getty Images:** p.192, 196–7, 198l, 246–7. **Graham Stark/Hulton Archive/Getty Images:** p.264tr. **Topical Press Agency/Getty Images:** pp.32, 33, 51r, 55, 58, 80r, 99, 116. **D. Venturelli/ WireImage/Getty Images:** p.304l. **Pierre Verdy/AFP/Getty Images:** pp.296l, 303. **Friedrich Walker/Imagno/Getty Images:** p.71. **Ian Walton/Getty Images:** p.122. **Ted West/ Central Press/Getty Images:** p.206. **Wesley/ Keystone/Getty Images:** p.212l. **Courtesy Special Collections, Gladys Marcus Library, Fashion Institute of Technology – Suny:** pp.25, 34, 41, 126, 137, 184, 188t. **© William P. Gottlieb, www.jazzphotos.com:** p.150l. **Courtesy of Jaeger and City of Westminster Archives:** p.67. **Courtesy of Kaleidoscope Consulting/Photo Anthony Goicolea:** p.312. **Courtesy of Kaleidoscope Consulting/Photo Marcelo Krasilcic:** p.313. **Courtesy of Nick Knight:** p.299. **Danjaq/EON/UA/The Kobal Collection:** p.222. **Live Entertainment/The Kobal Collection:** pp.238–9. **MGM/The Kobal Collection:** pp.216–17. **Riama-Pathe/The Kobal Collection:** p.219. **Spelling/Goldberg/ The Kobal Collection:** p.232. **Universal TV/ The Kobal Collection:** pp.234, 235. **Warner Bros./The Kobal Collection:** pp.88, 224, 227l. **Courtesy of Niall McInerney:** pp.276, 295r, 296r. **Courtesy of Iain McKell:** pp.245, 260, 261, 271tr, 272, 273. **Mary Evans Picture Library:** pp.31, 37tl, 46l. **Mary Evans Picture Library/ Anthony Lipmann:** p.90r. **Courtesy The Irene Lewisohn Costume Reference Library, The Costume Institute, The Metropolitan Museum of Art:** pp.28, 35tl, 35tr, 42–3, 45r, 103, 117l, 118bl, 119, 121. **Mirrorpix:** p.205r. **Moviestore Collection:** pp.214, 221, 230. **Museo di Arte Moderna e Contemporanea di Trento e Rovereto:** pp.72, 77. **Museo del Tessuto/ Courtesy of Elisabetta Seeber:** p.74. **Museo Nacional Centro de Arte Reina Sofia, Madrid/ © L & M SERVICES B.V. The Hague 20081107:** p.81. **Museum of London:** p.156b. **© National Portrait Gallery, London:** p.14, 44. **© Reserved/Collection National Portrait Gallery, London:** p.66. **© Estate of Russell Westwood/National Portrait Gallery, London:** p.156t. **© Lewis Morley Archive/National Portrait Gallery, London:** p.190l. **© Edward Lucie-Smith/National Portrait Gallery, London:** p.213. **Norman Parkinson Archive:** p.170. **Police Archives, Paris:** p.144. **Press Association:** p.149. **John G Byrne/PYMCA:** p.249b. **Ted Polhemus/PYMCA:** p.263. **David Swindells/PYMCA:** p.271tl. **Janette Beckman/ PYMCA:** p.280. **© Rennie Ellis Photographic Archive:** pp.187b, 203, 249t. **Rex Features:** p.200. **Albert Ferreira/Rex Features:** p.293t. **GLOBE/Rex Features:** pp.178, 201. **SNAP/Rex Features:** p.57. **Ray Stevenson/Rex Features:** p.255. **Richard Young/Rex Features:** p.262, 289t. **RMN © Succession Picasso/DACS 2009:** p.68t. **Rodchenko © DACS 2009:** p.78. **Roger-Viollet/ Topfoto:** pp.64, 80l, 146. **Ronald Grant Archive:** pp.92br, 193, 218, 223, 237. **Courtesy of Paolo Roversi:** p.287. **Photo Scala, Florence:** p.75. **Stapleton Collection:** pp.18, 35b, 104l. **Courtesy of Terence Spencer:** p.191. **Kharbine Tapabor:** p.145. **Topfoto © 2000 Topham Picturepoint:** p.36. **Topfoto © 1999 Topham Picturepoint:** p.37b. **Topfoto © 2002 Topham Picturepoint:** p.199. **© V&A Images:** 100b, 118br, 180, 187t, 203br, 264tl.

ACKNOWLEDGEMENTS

Dedicated to my father
Patrick Stuart-Williams
1909–2008

I am grateful to Laurence King, Helen Evans and John Jervis at Laurence King Publishing for their unfailing enthusiasm throughout the long process of writing this book – I hope their patience has been rewarded. Thanks also to Zoë Bather at Studio8 for her fantastic book design; Heather Vickers for her dogged perseverance and skill at picture research; Claire Gouldstone for her initial work on the project; Jennifer Jeffries at Getty for being so excited and getting me started; and Alex Fury at SHOWstudio for his invaluable suggestions and research.

I would also like to thank Marion Treasure, Steven Martin, Dr John Harvey, Philip and Liz de Bay at The Stapleton Collection, Fraser Leggat at Imprint, Tim Glazier of Herbert Johnson, Rio Ali at Burberry, Cassandra Robinson Brown at Austin Reed, Beatrice Behlen and Anna Wright at the Museum of London, Susan North, Orielle Cullen and Clemency Wright at the Victoria & Albert Museum. In New York, special thanks are due to Shawn Waldron and Jeana Evans at Condé Nast, Meryl Rothstein at *Esquire* magazine, Stéphane Houy-Towner and Harold Koda at the Metropolitan Museum of Art, Tabitha Hanslick-Nguyen, Professor N.J. Wolfe and Andrew Taylor at the Fashion Institute of Technology, and Mari Fujiuchi at Kaleidoscope Consulting. Also, for all her help, thank you to Elisabetta Barisoni of the Museo di arte moderna e contemporanea di Trento e Rovereto.

Many photographers have been generous in supplying images. I am very grateful to Kurt Marcus, Martin Brading, Jason Evans, Nick Knight, David Drebin, Paolo Roversi, Iain McKell and Niall McInerney.

Special thanks are due to Alistair O'Neill, Senior Research Fellow at Central Saint Martins, whose advice was always inspirational and productive. Shaun Cole, Research Fellow at The London College of Fashion, also kindly provided invaluable comments.

I am indebted to Noel B. Chapman for his help and generosity, and to Jack Slayford-Smith, Oscar Eavis and Rama Wieland, stylish young men all, who answered some of my more obscure queries.

As always, my family was tremendously supportive: Bonnie, Ophelia and, most of all, my husband Glen, without whose encouragement and patience I could not have managed. Finally I want to thank my father to whom this book is dedicated. Always elegant, even at the age of 98, he truly understood the meaning of style.